The Kogod Library of Judaic Studies
6

Messiahs and Resurrection in *The Gabriel Revelation*

By

Israel Knohl

מכון שלום הרטמן
SHALOM HARTMAN INSTITUTE

continuum

Published by Continuum

The Tower Building, 11 York Road, London SE1 7NX

80 Maiden Lane, Suite 704, New York, NY 10038

www.continuumbooks.com

British Library Cataloguing-in-Publication Data

A catalogue record for this book is available from the British Library

Typeset by Free Range Book Design & Production Limited

Printed and bound in Great Britain by Athenaeum Press Ltd.

ISBN-10: 0–8264-4669–8 (hardback)

0–8264-2507–0 (paperback)

ISBN-13: 978–0-8264–4669-5 (hardback)

978–0-8264–2507-2 (paperback)

Dedication

To my wife Dalia and my children:
Shay, Tal-Shahar and Orr.

Contents

Preface

The dramatic discovery of the apocalyptic text known as *Hazon Gabriel* or *The Gabriel Revelation* is a turning point in our understanding of the birth of Christianity. This book is the first broad scholarly work dedicated to this text.

Dr. David Jeselsohn, the owner of the stone on which this text is written, kindly enabled me to read the inscription in his house and also to use the photocopies published in the book.

The first editors of the text of *The Gabriel Revelation*, Dr. Ada Yardeni and Dr. Benjamin Elitzur have kindly shared their knowledge with me.

The writing of this book was made possible by the constant support of the Shalom Hartman Institute and its directors Rabbi Prof. David Hartman and Rabbi Dr. Donniel Hartman.

Parts of the book were translated faithfully by Orr Scharf and Gila Fine. Laura Major has done excellent work in editing the book.

My thanks are due to all of them.

Israel Knohl,
Yehezkel Kaufmann Chair in Bible Studies,
The Hebrew University, Jerusalem

Introduction

The Gabriel Revelation is an apocalyptic text dated to the turn of the Common Era. The dramatic finding of the apocalyptic text *The Gabriel Revelation* should change the way we view the historical Jesus and the birth of Christianity. It provides the key to understanding the roots of Jesus' messianic conception.

The text, first published in April 2007, was inscribed with ink in Hebrew over a large stone. It was discovered around the year 2000 in Jordan near the eastern shore of the Dead Sea. The authenticity of the stone was recently evaluated and confirmed by Prof. Yuval Goren of the archeology department at Tel-Aviv University. His research on this topic is expected to be published soon in the *Israel Exploration Journal.*[1] Prof. M. Bar Asher of the Hebrew University studied the language and the grammar of the text. His conclusions, soon to be published,[2] are that the text is authentic and that it was written around the turn of the Common Era. Similar conclusions with regard to the authenticity and the date have been reached by Dr. Ada Yardeni, who studied the script of the text.

According to Yuval Goren's examination, the stone probably comes from the area east of the small peninsula on the eastern side of the Dead Sea. We have evidence that Jews lived in this area during this period. This assumption is supported by the information that came from a reliable source in the antiquities market. According to this source, the stone was first sold to an antiquities dealer in the Karak area. Karak is the major city close to this area of the Dead Sea.

As stated above, the linguistic patterns and the shape of the script of *The Gabriel Revelation* indicate that it was written towards the end of the first century BCE – around the time of Jesus' birth. Thus *The Gabriel Revelation* is a pre-Christian text. *The Gabriel Revelation* centers on two

[1] Y. Goren, 'Micromorphic Examination of the "Gabriel Revelation" Stone,' *Israel Exploration Journal* 58 (2008), 220–229.
[2] M. Bar Asher, 'On the Language of the Vision of Gabriel,' *Revue de Qumrane* 92 (2008), 492–524.

themes. The first half describes an eschatological war, in which the nations of the world besiege Jerusalem, expelling its residents from the city. God, in response, sends 'My servant David' to ask Ephraim – the Messiah son of Joseph – to place 'a sign,' presumably heralding the coming redemption. The text goes on to describe the vanquishing of the Antichrist and its forces of evil. God Himself appears together with His angels to defeat the enemies.

The second half of *The Gabriel Revelation* focuses on death and resurrection. God declares that the blood of those slain by the enemies will become the chariot in which they will ascend to Heaven. The text also refers to three leaders – 'shepherds' – sent by God to His people, who were killed in battle. The last paragraph cites the words of the Archangel Gabriel, ordering his interlocutor (who remains unknown) to return to life after three days: 'By three days, live.'

The text, as mentioned above, dates to the end of the first century BCE. Jewish and Roman sources confirm that at that time a foreign army waged war on Jerusalem. The year 4 BCE saw the death of King Herod – the despot who had killed his wife and three of his sons. A great revolt broke out in the aftermath of Herod's death. Led by three messianic leaders, the rebels sought to throw off the yoke of the Roman-backed Herodian monarchy. The rebellion, which originated in Jerusalem and quickly spread throughout the country, was brutally crushed by the Roman Army under the command of Varus, Legate of Syria: the Temple was partly burned, cities were destroyed, villages razed and thousands of Jews killed or sold to slavery.

Apparently, *The Gabriel Revelation* was composed in response to the Roman army's brutal suppression of the rebellion. Its author, seeking to raise the spirits of the people, announces that redemption is at hand: God will wage war on the enemies and deliver His people from their hands.

The text concludes with a scene of resurrection. Gabriel's order 'By three days, live' appears in the 80th line of the text. The following line states that a leader – a 'prince of the princes' – was put to death, his corpse turned to dung amid the rocky crevices. Who is the man resurrected by Gabriel?

That *The Gabriel Revelation* was discovered in Jordan, and dates to the end of the first century BCE, may serve to locate the time and place of the death of this 'prince of the princes.' He thus may be identified with some probability.

A comparison of Jewish and Roman sources from the period suggests that Simon was the most prominent leader of the 4 BCE rebellion. A tall, sturdy man who had previously worked in Herod's service, Simon flourished in Jordan; he proclaimed himself to be king, adorned himself with a crown and was accepted by his followers as a monarch, harbinger of their messianic hopes. After his soldiers were defeated in battle, Simon attempted to escape by way of a narrow ravine – only to be caught by his enemies who killed him on the spot. The 'prince of the princes' would therefore seem to be Simon, the leader of the rebellion who found his death in the rocky crevices of Jordan.

The Gabriel Revelation presumably expresses the messianic hope of Simon's followers; the stone on which the text was inscribed may well have been placed as a monument near the site of his death. Faced with the crisis of a failed revolt and the death of their messianic king, Simon's followers cultivated the belief that the slain leader was resurrected three days after his death by the Archangel Gabriel.

The text, like other texts of its time (which survived only in later adaptations), presents a Messiah quite different from the conventional messianic view: not the heroic son of David, but the suffering son of Joseph, who will die in battle and be resurrected three days later. The death of the Messiah son of Joseph is, according to this tradition, a necessary stage in the redemptive process. The sign of the Messiah's shed blood rising to the heavens, will hasten God's descent onto the Mount of Olives to avenge the shed blood and save His people.

The discovery of *The Gabriel Revelation*, then, reveals far more than the messianic hope of the 4 BCE rebels; its unusual portrayal of the Messiah sheds new light on Jesus' act of self-sacrifice. It seems that Jesus did indeed possess a messianic secret. The son of Joseph the carpenter of Nazareth probably believed himself to be the embodiment of the Messiah the son of Joseph. Inspired by such secret texts as *The Gabriel Revelation*, Jesus followed the path of the tortured and killed Messiah, who was believed to be resurrected by Gabriel on the third day and to have placed the sign of the coming of redemption and salvation.

* * *

The *Gabriel Revelation*, or in its Hebrew title *Hazon Gabriel*, is inscribed with ink on gray limestone, 93 x 37 cm in size. The stone had been broken into three parts that match one another and is brown in its lower part. The stone was acquired by Dr. David Jeselsohn of Zurich.

The stone is cut on one side, along which two columns are inscribed; each is 16 cm wide and approximately 75 cm in height. The columns are separated by a gap approximately 3.5 cm wide. The inscription contains 47 horizontal lines engraved with stylus, as well as four vertical lines demarcating the columns' borders. The text comprises 87 lines: 44 in the right-hand column and 43 in the left-hand column. The last two lines of the left-hand column are shorter than the rest, and their ending is marked by diagonal lines.

The text was only partially preserved and the first lines of the right-hand column are illegible. Hence, we do not know for certain if the text begins with the first line of the right-hand column, or whether it was preceded by text that has not survived. It is plausible that the complete composition was comprised of an additional stone or several stones.

No clear traces of cement or similar substances were found on the stone. It thus seems unlikely that the stone served as part of a construction.[3] The lower part's brown color seems to suggest that it had been covered by soil. Hence, it would be reasonable to assume that the stone was wedged in the ground, probably to function as a memorial. The fact that one of the two other examples of a non-engraved inscription on unplastered stones known to me is the Zoar gravestones, which were found in the same area, might support this assumption.[4] Zoar is located on the southern coast of the Dead Sea. It is true that the earliest of the Zoar gravestones date to the mid-fourth century CE, i.e. 350 years later than *The Gabriel Revelation*. It is still possible, however, that they attest to a practice that was carried on down the generations. The other example is a text written on a limestone, found in the Qumran excavations near the western

---

[3]   Prof. Yuval Goren of Tel-Aviv University has reached this conclusion after examining the stone
[4]   See, S. Stern and H. Misgav, 'Four Additional Tombstones from Zoar,' *Tarbiz* 74 (2004): 137–152 (Heb.).

side of the Dead Sea.[5] This text was written at about the same time as *The Gabriel Revelation.*

As stated above, according to the tests conducted by Prof. Yuval Goren, the stone comes from an area near the eastern shore of the Dead Sea. We may thus see the writing with ink on stone as a local custom that prevailed around the shores of the Dead Sea.

The text of *The Gabriel Revelation* was first published by A. Yardeni and B. Elitzur.[6] Yardeni has dated the script of *The Gabriel Revelation* to the late first century BCE or early first century CE.[7] This estimate provides us only with the latest possible date for the composition of *The Gabriel Revelation,* since the surviving inscription may have been copied from an earlier text. Yardeni and Elitzur also determine, however, based on the text's language, that it was composed 'around the end of the first century BCE.'[8] We can hence assume that *The Gabriel Revelation* was composed and written around the turn of the Common Era. Since Gabriel is mentioned as a speaker in various lines of the composition, Yardeni and Elitzur have suggested naming it *Hazon Gabriel* – Gabriel's prophecy.[9]

Yardeni and Elitzur's transcription and reading of the text is impressive. In the summer of 2007, I read and made photocopies of the text in Zurich. Dr. David Jeselsohn also kindly provided me with various photocopies of the inscription that had been taken in the past. My transcription and reading of the text are based on the inspection of these materials and diverge from Yardeni and Elitzur on several points. My reading is offered in the first chapter of this book, followed by an English translation and commentary.

The second chapter is devoted to a general discussion of *The Gabriel Revelation:* structure, themes, biblical context, dating and provenance. In the third chapter I study the figure of the Antichrist in *The Gabriel Revelation* and related texts, while the final chapter focuses on *The Gabriel Revelation* and the birth of Christianity.

---

[5] See, J. B. Humbert and J. Gunneweg, *Khirbet Qumran et 'Ain Feshkha,* Vol. 2 (Fribourg: Academic Press Fribourg, 2003), 360–362.

[6] A. Yardeni and B. Elitzur, 'Document: A First-Century BCE Prophetic Text Written on a Stone: First Publication,' *Cathedra* 123 (2007): 55–66 (Heb).

[7] Yardeni and Elitzur, 162–166.

[8] *Ibid.,*156.

[9] *Ibid.,*162.

Chapter 1

The Gabriel Revelation:
Text, Translation and Commentary

The following presents my reading of the text of *The Gabriel Revelation*. As mentioned in the introduction, I read and made photocopies of the text in Zurich at the house of Dr. David Jeselsohn. He also provided me with various photocopies of the inscription that had been taken in the past. My transcription and reading of the text are based on the inspection of these materials. I have noted all the places in which my reading differs from that of the first editors, Yardeni and Elitzur. Broken or ambiguous letters are underlined. The English translation includes only full words; it does not indicate single letters.

1 [　　　　　　　　　　] מר̲..וצץ̲ ¹ [

2 [　　　　　　　　] יהרה̲ [?]...[²

3] 　　　　[ע] 　 [ב

4 [　　　] כ̲י כן אמ̲ר̲ יה̲וה̲[אר̲ש̲תי̲]ד̲ ל̲י̲ג̲ן ³

5 [　　　　　　　　　　] [.. ...] 5

6 ואגידה̲ ... ת ... ע ⁴ [

7 [ ] בני̲ ישראל̲ . ב̲..[?].ב̲] 　[?]..[ש̲..ל̲.

8 בנדודי̲ ⁵ [?] ל̲..ל̲..ל̲]

9 [ ] דבר יהו]ה̲[....פ̲ר̲......] ...[קו̲..ר̲ ⁶

10 [....[..יד̲... ל̲ב̲... ...תים שאל̲ת...[?]

11 [?]יהוה אתה שאלני כן אמר אלהים צבאות

12 [ ]..נ̲י מביתי ישראל ואגדה בגדלות ירושלם

13 [ ] אמר יהוה אל̲הי̲ ישראל הנה כו̲ל הגאים

---

¹ Yardeni and Elitzur read ד̲....... ... [.
² Yardeni and Elitzur read [ ]..ה̲.[?] ...[.
³ Yardeni and Elitzur read ....ארס̲.[ ]י̲כ̲ן [..
⁴ Yardeni and Elitzur read [.]י̲...[ ]..מ̲ל̲[ ]...ח̲[?]..ז̲ .הו. .ה̲. []..
⁵ Yardeni and Elitzur read [ ] בנ̲...ד [?]. ל̲..[?].ל̲ [ ]ל̲[ ].ד̲א̲.[?]
⁶ Yardeni and Elitzur read the last letter as ד̲.

‫... יַחַנ[נו] עַל ירושלם רן [ ] ומתוכ[בן]ה] מַוג נ[לים] .....[7]‬

‫15 אחת שתין שלוש ארבעין נביאין והשבין‬

‫16[ו]החסידין עבדי דוד בקש מן לפני אפרים[8]‬

‫17[וי]שים האות אני מבקש מן לפנך כי אמר‬

‫18 יהוה צבאות אלהי ישראל גני מבוכרים[9]‬

‫19 קדשה לישראל לשלשת ימין תדע כי אמר‬

‫20 יהוה אלהים צבאות אלהי ישראל נשבר הרע‬

‫21 מלפני הצדק שאלני ואגיד לכה מה הצמח‬

‫22 הרע הוה לובנסד[10] אתה עומד המלאך הוא‬

‫23 בסמכך[11] אל תירה[12] ברוך כבוד יהוה אלהים מן‬

‫24 מושבו עוד מעט קיטוט היא ואני מרעיש את‬

‫25 ...השמים וְאת הארץ הנה כבוד יהוה אלהים‬

‫26 צבאות אלהי ישראל אלה המרכבות שבע‬

‫27 [ע]ַל שער ירושלם ושערי יהודה ינחוּ[13] למען‬

‫28 שלושה[14] מלאכה מיכאל ולכול האחרין בקשו‬

‫29 אילכם[15] כן אמר יהוה אלהים צבאות אלהי‬

‫30 ישראל אחד שנין שלושה ארבעה חמשה ששה‬

‫31 [שב]ְעָה אל מלאכה ..... מה זו אמר הצץ‬

‫32 [ ].....ל.ד.פכ........ וַאלוף השני‬

‫33 שמר על ירושלם ...... שלושה בגדלות‬

‫34 [והו. ד. שלושה[16]] [..והו[ן?] .ד.ך‬

‫35 [ ]...ן. שראה איש ...עובד[17]] [...‬

‫36 שהוא שבו.] [שסמן מירושלם[18]‬

‫37..אני על.אי..[?] אפר[19] ואות גלות ..‬

---

[7] Yardeni and Elitzur read ...ג.... .מ.. .ושמתוב.. ‫עַל ירושלם‬.

[8] For the reading of this word see below, pages 9–10.

[9] While Yardeni and Elitzur read the words as ‫גנים.וכרים‬, the broken letter after ‫גני‬ may be a medial ‫מ‬ (for the shape of the ‫ב‬ of ‫מבוכרים‬ see the ‫ב‬ in ‫השבין‬, line 15).

[10] The editors also suggest the possibility of other readings; I believe this one is the correct reading. See commentary below.

[11] Yardeni and Elitzur read ‫בסמכך‬. My reading of ‫בסמכך‬ is supported by Psalms 54:6: ‫אדני בסמכי נפשי‬.

[12] Yardeni and Elitzur read ‫תורה‬ – see commentary (below).

[13] Yardeni and Elitzur read ‫ין.‬.

[14] Yardeni and Elitzur omit this word altogether.

[15] Yardeni and Elitzur read ‫ילכ..‬. In my view, the first letter is quite clearly ‫א‬. The ‫ם‬ at the end of the word is admittedly less certain; the two lines, however, form a triangle, similar in shape to the lower part of the ‫ם‬ in lines 27, 38 and 39.

[16] Yardeni and Elitzur read ‫לו...‬.

[17] Yardeni and Elitzur read ‫עובד וין‬.[...

[18] Yardeni and Elitzur read ‫מירושלם‬.

[19] Yardeni and Elitzur read ‫אבר. אות גלות‬ (for the shape of the ‫פ‬ in ‫אפר‬ see ‫לפנך‬, line 17).

38 ‏[א]ות גלות. ‏<u>צל‏</u> י.ל אלהים ‏<u>עון‏</u> או. ‏<u>וראו‏</u>[20]

39 ‏ג....א...[‏]ירושלם אמר יהוה

40 ‏.........א.ל .... ‏<u>למלא טחבו רוב ירח</u>..[21]

41 ‏] ‏דם שירם הצפוני[22]

42 ‏] ‏<u>דראון‏</u> הנגע . בכול[23]

43 ‏] ‏[ב אלהים][24]

44 ‏] ‏[ש[?]

Col. 2

45 ‏] [

46 ‏] ‏]י[[

47 ‏] ‏]י[[

48 ‏] ‏.. ל ..ע[

49 ‏] ‏] ..ד.. [‏ד. ך[

50 ‏] [

51 ‏] ‏עמך דרעוך[[

52 ‏ן ‏<u>הנמ‏</u>‏<u>לא‏</u>‏<u>כים‏</u>] ‏] מן..על[‏].דור[

53 ‏.ל.ש ומחר ל...‏<u>ינחו‏</u>...‏<u>גדל‏</u>.. .. שג..[25]

54 ‏[ל]שלשת ‏<u>ימין‏</u> זה שאמ[רתי][26] ‏הוא

55 ‏אל‏<u>ה‏</u>] [..א] ‏[של].. ‏] ...[‏]..[‏[

56 ‏ראו נא ‏<u>הצפ‏</u>[וני] ‏<u>חו‏</u>[נה][27] ‏] [

---

20 Yardeni and Elitzur read ‏וראה‏.ן.א...ע אלהים .[‏]. ‏<u>צל‏</u> . ‏אתגלות‏.

21 Yardeni and Elitzur read ‏<u>צבאות‏</u>..א.ל.. .. ....ל.. ‏חנארו.ורח. [?]. My reading differs from theirs in several points: (1) the letters after the ‏ל‏ in the middle of the line are, according to my reading, ‏מלאט‏; (2) after the ‏ח‏, on which our readings agree, Yardeni and Elitzur read ‏נא‏, while I read ‏בו‏; (3) the following letters are, according to both readings, ‏רו‏ – after which there is another letter that Yardeni and Elitzur omit but I read as ‏ב‏.; (4) Yardeni and Elitzur then read ‏ורח‏ which, in my view, should be slightly corrected to ‏ירח‏. Thus, my reading presents the sequence of letters ‏למלאטחבורובירח‏, which I suggest to read as ‏למלא טחבו רוב ירח‏.

22 Yardeni and Elitzur read ‏שירם‏ ..... ‏דם‏ [I believe the last word, not read by Yardeni and Elitzur, is ‏הצפוני‏. The shape of the ‏פ‏ is similar to that of the ‏פ‏ in ‏לפני‏, line 16. The ‏צ‏ is broken; while the top half is not as well preserved as the bottom half, one can notice the traces of the upper right line typical to this letter (see the shape of the ‏צ‏ in ‏הצדק‏, line 21).

23 Yardeni and Elitzur read ‏בכל‏ .‏הנגי‏. ‏ן.א‏ .[. In my view, the letters ‏דר‏ should be read before the ‏א‏, and the letters ‏ון‏ after it (there are, it should be noted, exceptionally wide gaps between the last three letters of ‏דראון‏). Although Yardeni and Elitzur read the second word as ‏הנגי‏, my reading – based on the clearly legible rounded right-hand line of the last letter – has it as ‏הנגע‏.

24 Yardeni and Elitzur read ‏..[... ב ש.ו‏.

25 Yardeni and Elitzur read ‏שג‏[‏]..[‏].[‏]. ‏ה‏...‏ומחר‏ ‏עמו‏ ‏על‏.

26 Yardeni and Elitzur read ‏] ‏.[‏שאמ‏ זה ‏ימין‏ ‏שלשת‏[‏] .[‏הוא‏.

27 Yardeni and Elitzur read ‏ה.צ‏.... ..[. According to my reading, there is an additional letter between the ‏ה‏ and ‏צ‏, after which one may discern traces of a ‏פ‏ and of two other letters – probably ‏ני‏. It is then possible to distinguish the letters ‏וח‏.

57 סתום דם‎[28] טבחי ירושלם כי אמר יהוה צבא[ות]

58 אלהי ישראל כן אמר יהוה צבאות אלהי

59 ישראל מא.. ל.. ... אל....].[   ].[   ]ד..[?]

60 ה.לני .ך יחמול ..רחמו קרבני[ן][29] ..]   [

61].. [   ]ל אשריא...... תץ ש ... [?]

62 בת.ל   א.   א..ע..נ[30]   ]   [

63 א.[ ]   אב.[?].א[ ]...[ ].[ ].[

64 [ ]..[ ]   [ה.]חביב ...ל ... [

65 שלושה קדושי העולם מן מק.]   [

66].[ ].ו שלום אמר עליך אנחנו ב[טו]חין]   [

67] בשר לו על דם זו המרכבה שלהן ..ל.

68 אוהבין רבים ליהוה צבאת אל<ה>י ישראל

69 כה אמר יהוה צבאת אלהי ישראל .מ.......

70 נביאים שלחתי אל עמי של[ושה רועי אומר][31]

71 שראיתי ברכ. ל..לך דבר .ברן].[?].ב...[

72 המקום למ[ען] דוד עבד יהוה]   א.[ ].. [

73 את השמים ואת הארץ ברוך......]   [

74 אנשים עושה חסד לאלפים מ.... חסד .[]

75 שלושה רועין יצאו לישראל .ל ...[ ]..[

76 אם יש כהן אם יש בני קדושים...ה].. [

77 מי אנכי אני גבריאל המל.כי .לי ..מל]   [

78 תצילם נבי..ם גרי.ם[32]לשו[ת].[33]   ].ב..[

79 מל[פ]ניך שלושה הא[ות]ות שלושה ... אק]   [

80 לשלושת ימין האיה[34] אני גבריאל ג[ו]זר[עלי]ך[35]

81 שר השרין דומ[ן][36] ארו[בות] צרים אן .[ ].א...[?]

---

[28] While Yardeni and Elitzur are hesitant regarding the reading of תום דם, I find it unquestionable.

[29] Yardeni and Elitzur read [?]..ל שק. תן..הלני רוח הנרא [   ]. However, the letter they read as ר in רוח clearly extends below the line and should be read as ך. After a short gap, the letters יחמו are easily detectable, followed by: (1) an ambiguous ול, (2) two illegible letters, (3) a distinct רה, (4) a unclear מו, (5) a ק and (6) a possible רב.

[30] Yardeni and Elitzur read [ ]..[?].ד ב..[   ].בה.א

[31] Even though Yardeni and Elitzur read ואני אומר, I find the word before last to be unmistakably רועי (note the resemblance between the ו of רועי and the ו of both the previous word שלושה and of שלום, line 66). According to this reading, the grammatical sentence begins with the word שלחים, making נביאים the final word of the (missing) short sentence begun in the final part of line 69.

[32] Yardeni and Elitzur read גר..ם.

[33] Yardeni and Elitzur read לשות.ן.

[34] Yardeni and Elitzur read ה.... For the justification of my reading, see commentary.

[35] See commentary.

[36] See commentary.

82 לְמַרְאוֹת ה...לשׁנם מן [....] [מן נשׁל...ה וְאַהֲבֵי³⁷ ג.מ. [?]
83 לי מן שׁלושׁה הקטן שׁל קחתי אני גבריאל
84 יהוה צבאת אלהַנָ֫יֵן יִשַׁ֫[ראל] [ ] [
85 אז תעמדו א.[].. ל [ ] [........א [?]
86 יול. א. .....³⁸\
87 ב.... עַלם \ם\

Col. 1

1. [   ] ……..
2. [   ] Lord
3. [   ] . [   ] .
4. [f]or th[us sa]id the Lo[rd] I have betr[oth]ed you
to me, garden
5. [   ]… ..[
6. and I will talk …. …. [
7. [   ] children of Israel …. [?]…[   ] …[   ] ….
8. son of David [?] ……[
9. [   ] the word of the Lor[d]
10. [   ] …. ….. ….. ….. you have asked … [?]
11[?] Lord you have asked me, so said the God of Hosts
12 [   ] .. from my house Israel and I will talk about the greatness of
Jerusalem
13 [Thus] said the Lord, God of Israel, now all the nations
14 … enc[amp] on Jerusalem and from it are exi[led]
15 one two three forty Prophets and the elders
16 and the Hasidim. My servant David, ask of Ephraim
17 [that he] place the sign; (this) I ask of you. For thus said
18 the Lord of Hosts, the God of Israel, my gardens are ripe,
19 My holy thing for Israel. By three days you shall know, for thus
said
20 the Lord of Hosts, the God of Israel, the evil has been broken
21 before righteousness. Ask me, and I shall tell you, what is this
22 wicked branch, plastered white. You are standing, the angel
23 is supporting you. Do not fear. Blessed is the glory of the Lord
God from

---

³⁷ Yardeni and Elitzur read וה.ב.
³⁸ Yardeni and Elitzur read \ …. …ל…

24 his seat. In a little while, I will shake

25 .. the heavens and the earth. Here is the glory of the Lord God

26 of Hosts, the God of Israel, These are the seven chariots

27 at the gate of Jerusalem and the gates of Judea they will re[st] for

28 my three angels, Michael and all the others, look for

29 your power. So said of the Lord God of Hosts, the God

30 of Israel. One two three four five six

31 [se]ven for my angels..... what is this? He said, the frontlet

32 .... [   ] .... and the second chief

33 watches on.. Jerusalem ...... three in the greatness

34.................. three [   ] .....

35 [   ] .... . that he saw a man ... works [

36 that he .... [   ] that a sign from Jerusalem

37 I on ...[ ] ashes and a sign of exile ..

38 [s]ign of exile .... God sin ... and see

39 ... ... [   ] Jerusalem said the Lord

40 .... That his mist will fill most of the moon

41[   ] blood that the northerner would become maggoty

42. [   ]abhorrence the diseased spot . in all

43 [   ] . God [

44 [   ] . [?]

Col. 2 (There are no legible words before line 51)

51 with you (or: your nation) ....

52 .. the angels [   ] from ... on [   ] ..

53 ... and tomorrow to ... they will rest ... big .. .. ..

54[by] three days this is what [I have] said   He

55. these are [

56 please see the north[erner] enca[mps] [

57 Seal up the blood of the slaughtered of Jerusalem. For thus said the Lord of Hos[ts]

58 the God of Israel, So said the Lord of Hosts the God of

59 Israel [

60 ... He will have pity .. His mercy are ne[ar]

61 [   ] blessed ? ...

62 daughter ? ...

63 ...

64 [ ] ...[ ] beloved ?

65 Three holy ones of the world from.... [   ]

66 [ ] **shalom** he said, in You we tr<u>ust</u> ... [?]

67 Announce him of blood, this is their chariot.

68 Many are those who love the Lord of Hosts, the God of Israel

69 Thus said the Lord of Hosts, the God of Israel ....[?]

70 prophets. I sent to my people my th<u>ree</u> <u>shepherds</u>. <u>I will say</u> (?)

71 that I have seen bless[ing]... ..... Go say(?)

72 The place <u>for</u> David the servant of the Lord [   ]...[ ] .. [   ]

73 The heaven and the earth, blessed ...... [   ]

74 <u>men.</u> Showing steadfast love to thousands .... steadfast love. [   ]

75 Three shepherds went out for Israel ... [ ]...

76 If there is a priest, if there are sons of holy ones ....[ ]

77 <u>Who am I</u>? I am Gabriel .... [   ]

78 You will rescue them.............. <u>for two</u> [   ] ...[ ]

79 from be<u>fore</u> of you the three si[g]ns three .. [   ]

80 By three days, live, I Gabriel <u>com</u>[mand] <u>yo</u>[u],

81 prince of the princes, the d<u>ung</u> of the rocky crevices [   ].... ..[ ]

82 to the <u>visions</u> (?) <u>... their tongue</u> (?) [   ] ... <u>those who love me</u>

83 to me, from the three, the small one that I took, I Gabriel

84 Lord of Hosts G<o>d of Is[rael] [

85 then you will stand ...

86 ...   /

87 ... <u>world</u> ? /

Commentary

Line 4: 'f]or th[us sa]id the Lo[rd] I have betr[oth]<u>ed you to me,</u>
<u>garden</u>' – The reading is far from certain. The idea of Israel as
betrothed to the Lord is based on Hosea 2:21–22. Similarly, the word
'garden' may serve as a metaphor for Israel, the spouse of God (see
Song of Songs 4:12: 'A garden locked is my sister, my bride').

Line 8: 'son of David' – The reading of the Hebrew term בנדוד is inconclusive. In the case of a common expression such as בן דוד, it is not unusual for the two words to be compounded into one.[39] 'Son of David' is a common messianic title (see, for instance, Psalms of Solomon 17:21 and Matt. 9:27). David is mentioned in line 16 as עבדי דוד 'My servant David,' and in line 72 as דוד עבד יהוה 'David, the servant of the Lord.'

Line 10: 'you have asked' – The subject is not clear from the immediate context. It seems that the verb שאל 'to ask' is used in *The Gabriel Revelation* as a dialogical literary device (see, אתה שאלני 'You have asked me,' line 11 and שאלני ואגיד לכה 'Ask me, and I shall tell you,' line 21). Interestingly, a similar use of שאל may be found in the beginning of *Sefer Zerubbabel*, a book closely linked to *The Gabriel Revelation*;[40] the dialogue between God and Zerubbabel, the recipient of the vision, opens with the words שאל ואגידה לך 'Ask and I shall tell you.'[41] This expression, repeated several times in *Sefer Zerubbabel*,[42] is unparalleled in ancient Jewish literature. In *The Gabriel Revelation*, however, it appears both here and in line 21 שאלני ואגיד לכה. This linguistic linkage may attest to a direct connection between these two compositions.

Lines 11–12: 'so said the God of Hosts [   ] .. from my house Israel' – In addition to being God's spouse (line 4), Israel is presented as God's house. This metaphor is never mentioned explicitly in the Hebrew Bible, though one might recall Zechariah 9:8: 'Now I will encamp at my house as a guard, that none shall march to and fro, no oppressor shall again overrun them.' At the beginning of the verse in Zechariah God refers to His house, but goes on to speak about 'them.' Hence, we may infer that Israel ('them'), in this verse, is the house that God guards ('my house').

[39] Writings of this period are replete with such expressions (see, for example, the discussion of לובנסר, line 22 and the spelling of עינגדה, n. 49).
[40] See M. Himmelfarb, 'Sefer Zerubbabel,' in *Rabbinic Fantasies: Imaginative Narratives from Classical Hebrew Literature*, eds. D. Stern and M. J. Mirsky (Philadelphia: Jewish Publication Society, 1990), 67–90.
[41] See, Y. Even Shmuel, *Midreshei Geulah*, 2nd edn. (Jerusalem and Tel-Aviv, 1954), 379, 383, 385.
[42] *Ibid.*, 380, 384, 386, 387.

Line 12: 'I will talk about the greatness of Jerusalem' – For גדלות 'the greatness' see 1 Chronicles 17:19 (alternatively, we may read this word as in Jeremiah 33:3). The verse probably serves as an introduction to the miraculous salvation of Jerusalem, depicted in the following lines.

Lines 13–4: 'now all the nations ... enc[amp] on Jerusalem' – See Zechariah 14:2: 'For I will gather all the nations against Jerusalem to battle.' The unusual spelling גאים, instead of the more conventional גוים, is paralleled in the spelling גואים in the Dead Sea Scrolls and הגואין in one of the Bar Kokhba letters.[43]

Line 14: 'and from it are exi[led]' – The reading [מוגלי[ם 'are exiled' is doubtful, but might be supported by Zechariah 14:2: 'half of the city shall go into exile.'

Lines 15–16: 'one two three forty Prophets and the elders and the Hasidim' – The Prophets נביאין are mentioned first, followed by the elders השבין (the word השבין can mean also 'those who return;' the context, however, suggests that it should be translated as 'the elders') and the Hasidim החסידין. Prophecy, for the author of *The Gabriel Revelation*, seems to be an existing phenomenon. The numbers in the verse 'one two three forty Prophets' add up to 46; according to the Talmudic tradition (*b. Megilah* 14a) 'forty eight prophets stood for Israel.' We cannot know for certain if 'Hasidim' refers to a specific group within the People of Israel.[44]

Lines 16–17: 'My servant David, ask of Ephraim' – Yardeni and Elitzur mark the letters ם, י, פ of אפרים as uncertain. In my view the פ is certain. One might compare the shape of this פ to the shape of the פ in the word מלפני in line 21. As for the י, in the original inscription the right part of this letter is seen very well (this is not represented

---

[43] See E. Qimron, *The Hebrew of the Dead See Scrolls* (Atlanta, GA: Scholars Press, 1986), 31 and n. 28.

[44] On the Hasidim in other Jewish writings of the period see: J. Kampen, *The Hasideans and the Origins of Pharisaism* (Atlanta: Scholars Press, 1988); S. Safrai, 'Jesus and Hasidim,' *Jerusalem Perspectives* 42–44 (1994): 3–22.

correctly in Yardeni and Elizur's transcription). The left side of this
letter is missing due to a diagonal crack in the stone. For the same
reason, we cannot see the left side of the letter ם, but the general shape
of this letter is clear. Thus, even though the two final letters of this
word were partially damaged due to the crack, in my view, the reading
of the word as אפרים (Ephraim) is certain. The Hebrew phrase
עבדי דוד בקש מן לפני אפרים has two possible readings: (1)
God addresses his servant David, asking him to request something
of Ephraim, or (2) God states that His servant David has requested
something of Ephraim. The continuation of the passage confirms
the first possibility. Yardeni and Elitzur read the next line as
שים האות אני מבקש מן לפנך.[ ]. Hence, the plausible reconstruction
of the first word as וישים gives the following coherent reading:
עבדי דוד בקש מן לפני אפרים [וי]שים האות, אני מבקש מן לפנך
'My servant David, ask of Ephraim [that he] place the sign; (this) I
ask of you.' The Lord addresses David, asking him to request from
Ephraim to place a sign. The nature of the sign remains unclear.

Two biblical characters are mentioned in the verse: David and
Ephraim. In addition to designating the actual character, the
expression 'My servant David' appears in the Bible as a general term
for an eschatological leader (see Ezek. 34:23–24, 37:24–25). As for
Ephraim, the biblical Ephraim is the son of Joseph. Hence, 'My
servant David' and 'Ephraim' may well represent the Messiah son of
David and the Messiah son of Joseph mentioned in the Talmud. As
noted by Yardeni and Elitzur, the *Pesikta Rabbati* refers to the Messiah
who suffers in order to atone for Israel as 'Ephraim.'[45] In the Bible,
'Ephraim' is used primarily to denote northern Israel. I believe that
certain biblical verses are the basis of the image of Ephraim as a
suffering 'Son of God' or messianic figure: in Jeremiah 31:18, for
example, Ephraim declares: 'Thou hast chastened me, and I was
chastened' and is answered by God: 'Truly, Ephraim is a dear son to

---

[45] See *Pesikta Rabbati* 36 (ed. M. Ish-Shalom [Friedmann] 162–163). While it is true that
in the Dead Sea Scrolls 'Ephraim' is used as a term for the Pharisees, the name does
not seem to bear such a meaning in our text, which is completely devoid of Qumranic
terminology and sectarian polemic.

Me. A child that is dandled!'[46] A similar portrayal of Ephraim may be found in Hosea 11:1–8.

The tradition of the Messiah son of Joseph and his death appears in the Talmud (BT Sukkah 52a) and, at greater length, in *Sefer Zerubbabel.* Elsewhere I have argued that this tradition was established in the late first century BCE or the early first century CE.[47] *The Gabriel Revelation* confirms my assumption that the Messiah son of Joseph was already well known around the beginning of the Common Era.

Line 18: 'my gardens are ripe' – To understand the words 'my gardens,' I suggest we read them in light of Jesus' description of the Kingdom of God:

> The Kingdom of God is as if a man should scatter seed upon the ground, and should sleep and rise night and day, and the seed should sprout and grow... But when the grain is ripe, at once he puts in the sickle, because the harvest has come. (Mark 4:26–29)

God's gardens, having ripened, symbolize the Kingdom of God that is now ready for Israel.

Line 19: 'My holy thing for Israel' – The translation is based on the interpretation of the words קדשה לישראל as קדשי לישראל[48] (see Isaiah 57:13: 'and shall inherit my holy mountain').

'By three days you shall know' – The expression לשלשת ימים 'by three days' recurs in line 80 and may also be reconstructed in line 54. It appears three times in the Hebrew Bible (Exodus 19:15, Amos 4:4 and Ezra 10:8).

---

[46] Jer. 31:20 (according to the JPS translation). According to Fishbane, these verses depict Ephraim as both the suffering and beloved Son of God (see M. Fishbane, 'Midrash and Messianism: Some Theologies of Suffering and Salvation,' in *Toward the Millennium*, eds. Schaefer and M. R. Cohen (Leiden: Brill, 1998), 70–71.)

[47] See I. Knohl, 'On "the Son of God," Armilus and Messiah Son of Joseph,' *Tarbiz* 68 (1998): 13–38. (The article is in Hebrew with an English abstract.)

[48] The sound change of ī to ē, when the letter ה appears at the end of a word, is quite common in writings of this period. Thus, the place name עין גדי is spelled עינגדה. See H. M. Cotton and E. Qimron, 'XHev/ Se ar of 134 or 135', *JJS* 49 (1998): 110–111. (I am indebted to my friend Prof. Shlomo Naeh for drawing my attention to this possibility.)

Lines 20–21: 'the evil has been broken before righteousness' – The phrase is most probably based on the biblical prophecy of Gabriel against the wicked king: וּבְאֶפֶס יָד יִשָּׁבֵר 'but, by no human hand, he shall be broken' (Daniel 8:25).

Lines 21–22: 'Ask me, and I shall tell you, what is this wicked branch plastered white' – As Yardeni and Elitzur remark,[49] 'branch' is a typical messianic name. Jeremiah prophesies:

> Behold, the days are coming, says the Lord, when I will raise up for David a righteous branch, and he shall reign as king and deal wisely, and shall execute justice and righteousness [...] And this is the name by which he will be called: 'The Lord is our righteousness.' (Jeremiah 23:5)

In Jeremiah, the righteous branch is a distinguished king bearing the divine name 'the Lord is our righteousness.' Antithetically, the 'evil branch'[50] of *The Gabriel Revelation* is a wicked messianic king, a precursor to what would subsequently be termed the Antichrist.[51]

Known to us from apocalyptic works similar to *The Gabriel Revelation*,[52] the Antichrist is characteristically duplicitous, presenting himself as the Messiah and Redeemer while actually being the Devil's spawn, seeking to corrupt and lead astray.[53] This characterization may serve to elucidate an enigmatic word in our text. The term 'wicked branch' is immediately followed (1.22) by a word Yardeni and Elitzur had great difficulty reading and interpreting. The possibilities they offer are לוּבנסד, לִיבנסד, לוּבנסר, לִיבנסר, לִיבנסד, לוּבנסד, לוּבנסך, לִיבנסך.

[49] 157.
[50] Note the striking similarity between this phrase and עֵץ הָרֶשַׁע 'the tree of evil' in a Qumran document (which also references the Messiah מָשׁוּחַ בְּשֶׁמֶן מַלְכוּת 'anointed [Messiah] with the oil of kingship'); see E. Larson, '4Q Narrative A [4Q458],' *Qumran Cave 4, XXVI: Cryptic Texts, Discoveries in the Judean Desert* 36 (Oxford: Oxford University Press, 2000), 355–360.
[51] This evil messianic figure must be distinguished from the more conventional type of false messiah, who wishes to redeem Israel but cannot achieve this goal. Here, emphasis is laid upon the sheer wickedness of the would-be redeemer.
[52] See D. Flusser, *Judaism and the Origins of Christianity* (Jerusalem: Magnes Press, 1988), 207–213, 433–453; Knohl, 'On "the Son of God," Armilus and Messiah Son of Joseph.' 13–38.
[53] For the Antichrist as a pretender see A. Yarbro-Collins, *The Combat Myth in the Book of Revelation* (Missoula: Scholars Press, 1976), 166–167.

Closely examining the original inscription, I believe the first option is correct: לובנסד. This expression is not known elsewhere. I would like to suggest that it might be translated as 'white plaster' [לובן סיד] or 'plastered white' [לובן סוד]. This singular expression probably describes the duplicity of the evil branch, which, though wicked and corrupt, assumes the guise of the Messiah, pure and righteous ('whitewashed'). The New Testament uses similar terms to depict the hypocrisy of the wicked: the High Priest Ananias, who claims to judge Paul according to the Torah but has him beaten contrary to the law, is described by the latter as a whitewashed wall (Acts 23:3); Jesus likens the two-faced Pharisees, who have the appearance of righteousness but are steeped in hypocrisy, to whitewashed tombs full of uncleanliness (Matt. 23:27). While the spelling of לובנסד as a single word is exceptional and difficult, it might reflect the widespread use of the term at the time.[54] Semantically, it resembles the Greek κεκονιαμέvε, which appears in the above mentioned New Testament, and possibly draws upon similar popular expressions.[55] Another option is to see לובנסד as a Hebrew form of some loaned Greek or Latin word.

Lines 22–23: 'You are standing, the angel is supporting you' – Yardeni and Elitzur read כסמכך. As mentioned before, my reading בסמכך is supported by Psalms 54:6(4) אדני בסמכי נפשי 'the Lord is the upholder of my life.'

Line 23: 'Do not fear' – Yardeni and Elitzur read אל תורה 'to the Torah' which, in the given context, makes little sense. I propose the reading אל תירה, to be understood as אל תירא 'Do not fear.' The entire scene, I believe, is based on the description of Gabriel's revelation to Daniel:

So he came near where I stood; and when he came, I was frightened and fell upon my face. But he said to me, 'Understand, O son of man that the vision is for the time of the end.' As he was speaking to me, I fell into a deep sleep with my face to the ground; but he touched me and set me on my feet (Dan. 8:17–18).

---

[54] See the reconstruction of בנדוד, line 8.
[55] See E. Haenchen, *The Acts of the Apostles* (Oxford: Basil and Blackwell, 1971), 638.

Just as Daniel falls upon his face and Gabriel sets him on his feet, the recipient of the vision in *The Gabriel Revelation* is supported by an angel who helps him stand upright and calms him: 'You are standing, the angel is supporting you. Do not fear.'

Lines 23–24: 'Blessed is the glory of the Lord God from his seat' – See Ezek. 3:12. For the parallelism between ממקומו 'his place' in the biblical text and מן מושבו 'his place' here, see the parallelism in Isaiah 66:1: 'Heaven is my *throne* ... and what is the *place of my rest*.'

Lines 24–25: 'In a little while, I will shake .. the heavens and the earth' – See Haggai 2:6: 'Once again in a little while, I will shake the heavens and the earth and the sea and the dry land' (a verse used in the Talmud as a basis for an eschatological prediction; see BT.*Sanhedrin* 97b). As suggested by Yardeni and Elitzur (p. 162), the words מעט קיטוט correspond to the expression כמעט קט in Ezekiel 16:47. The form קיטוט is not found elsewhere.

Lines 25–26: 'Here is the glory of the Lord God of Hosts, the God of Israel' – The shaking of the earth serves as a sign for the appearance of God; see Zechariah 14:4–5.

Lines 26–28: 'These are the seven chariots on the gate of Jerusalem and the gates of Judea they will re[st] for my three angels' – According to Zechariah 14:5, God will come 'and all the holy ones with him.' Here too, God is accompanied by the angels who descend in chariots and rest at the gates of Jerusalem and Judea. The image of the chariots is probably based on Isaiah 66:15: 'For behold, the Lord will come in fire, and His chariots like a storm-wind, to render His anger in fury, and His rebuke with flames of fire.'

Line 28: Based on the syntax and on conventional sound changes,[56] I have translated the word מלאכה as מלאכי 'my angels,' both here and in line 31.

---

[56] In writings of the period it is not unusual for the sound ē to be read as the diphthong a̲y̲. See Cotton and Qimron, n. 48.

'Michael and all the others' – According to the book of Daniel, Michael is the prince of Israel who takes part in the war against the nation's enemies (Daniel 10:20–21). The other angel to take part in this war is described as the 'man clothed in linen' (Daniel 10:5) – most probably Gabriel.[57] Thus, two of the three angels accompanying the Lord seem to be Michael and Gabriel. The identity of the third remains unclear.

Lines 28–29: בקשו אילכם 'look for your power' – The reading of אילכם is uncertain. God appeals to the aforementioned angels to look for their strength. Judging by the wider context, the request is probably a call to the angels to gather their military forces and join God in His war against the enemies of Jerusalem and Judea. The image of the angels and their chariots fighting beside God is probably based on the verses of Zechariah 14:3–5.

Several biblical verses employ the word בקש to mean 'look for.' The word איל, in biblical context, can be understood as power or strength (see Psalms 88:4). Interestingly, we find an analogous expression in the *Oracles of Hystaspes,* an apocalyptic composition in many ways akin to *The Gabriel Revelation.*[58] The author of the *Oracles of Hystaspes* provides the following description of the eschatological war: 'and he [i.e. the messianic king] shall descend with company of angels ... and the power of the angels [*virtus angelorum*] shall deliver into the hands of the just, that multitude which has surrounded the mountain.'[59] Thus, according to the *Oracles of Hystaspes* the just men will be saved by the power of the angels (*virtus angelorum*) fighting against their enemies.

I would, furthermore, like to suggest that the author's unusual choice of the word איל, rather than the more conventional צבא or חיל, was perhaps motivated by his desire to play on the Greek word ἴλη or the Latin *ala alae*; the original meaning of the Latin *ala* is

[57] See J. J. Collins, *Daniel, Hermeneia* (Minneapolis: Fortress Press, 1993), 373.
[58] See the discussion in my article 'Studies in The Gabriel Revelation' *Tarbiz* 76 (2007): 1–26.
[59] Lactantius, *The Divine Institutes,* VII, 19, 5, ed. S. Brandt, CSEL, 19, I, ii (Prague, Vienna, Leipzig: 1890, N.Y.: 1965), 645. The English translation is after: *Ante-Nicene Fathers,* eds. A. Roberts and J. Donaldson, Vol. 7 (Peabody, MA: Hendrickson Publishers, 1994), 215.

'wing,' and later on it came to denote the cavalry unit in the legion flanks.[60] The Latin *ala* probably appears in Rabbinic literature in the Hebrew form אילת.[61]

Lines 30–31: 'One two three four five six [se]ven for my angels' – The numbers, written in the masculine form אחד שנין שלושה ארבעה חמשה ששה [שב]עה, seemingly do not refer to the aforementioned seven chariots (line 26), noted in the feminine form (שבע). If indeed בקשו אילכם has the secondary meaning of 'look for your cavalry,' these numbers may refer to the cavalry units that appear in a masculine form א[ילכם. Thus, the angels with the seven chariots will be accompanied by seven units of cavalry – חﺍֵﬥ, *ala, alae*. However, since in line 15 we have a transition from the feminine אחת שתין שלוש to the masculine ארבעין, one might argue that the author was indifferent to grammatical gender, and that the numbers here do in fact refer to the aforementioned seven chariots.

Line 31: 'what is this? He said, the frontlet' – The questioner, presumably, is God – the only speaker in the text thus far. In the reply, however, we are introduced to a different voice, a voice designated by the phrase אמר 'he said.' The phrase is repeated in line 66: אמר עליך אנחנו בטוחין 'he said, in You we trust,' in which the speaker there seems to be a human being professing his trust in God. This line, I believe, presents a similar situation. Responding to God's question מה זו 'what is this?,' a human voice answers: '(He said,) the frontlet.'

Who is God's interlocutor? Until now, the only human being addressed by God is the recipient of the vision: אתה עומד המלאך הוא בסמכך אל תירה 'You are standing, the angel is supporting you. Do not fear' (lines 22–23). Here too, it would seem, God is

---

60   See, 'alae,' *The Oxford Classical Dictionary* (Oxford: Oxford University Press, 1990), 33. These 'wings,' arguably, are mentioned in the Qumranic War Scroll 9:11. (See Y. Yadin, *The Scroll of the War of the Sons of Light and the Sons of Darkness* (Jerusalem, 1995), 312. (Heb.). See also Yadin's discussion, 176–177.)

61   See, ואילת צפירה מקפתו Mekhilta D'Rabbi Simon b. Jochai, ed. J. N. Epstein & E. Z. Melamed, 78 and the discussion of S. Kraus, *Persia and Rome in the Talmud and Midrash*, (Jerusalem: Mosad HaRav Kook, 1948), 182 (Heb.).

asking the recipient of the vision מה זו 'what is this?,' possibly pointing at the object in question [just as He does in a remarkably similar scene in Jeremiah 1, in which He asks the prophet: 'what do you see?' (Jeremiah 1:11, 13)]. While the Hebrew word זו, rather than זה, signifies an object of the feminine form, we have seen that the author of *The Gabriel Revelation* was not necessarily concerned with grammatical gender.

In response, the recipient of the vision says הציץ 'the frontlet,' probably referring to the object pointed out by God. As ציץ is a verb rather than a noun, we may assume that the word is actually a shorter form of הציץ. The word can be used to mean 'flower,' as in Isaiah 40:7: נבל ציץ 'the flower fades.' If that, however, was the case, the word ought to have appeared as the non-definite ציץ 'a flower,' rather than the definite הציץ '*the* flower.' The definite form seems to indicate a unique object, such as the golden frontlet worn by the high priest on his forehead, referred to in the Bible as ציץ (see Exodus 28:37[36], 39:30; Leviticus 8:9). We may therefore assume that the object in question is the high-priest's frontlet.

What links this dialogue to the angels described in the previous passage? The angels, descending in chariots to wage war against the enemies of Jerusalem, are led by Michael – the apparent commander-in-chief of the divine army. A similar description of the eschatological war may be found in the *Testament of Moses* (10:2): 'Then will be filled the hands of the messenger who is in the highest place appointed. Yea, he will at once avenge them of their enemies.'[62] Scholars have noted that the expression 'filled the hands' echoes the biblical term מלא ידים, a term describing the dedication to the priestly service (see Exodus 29:9, 32:29; Leviticus 8:33; Judges 17:5).[63] Thus, in the *Testament of Moses* (as in 11Q *Melchizedek*), the messenger is a unique character who combines the mission of avenger with the role of high priest. Here too, it would seem, Michael (depicted in other sources as the high priest

---

[62] See J. Priest, 'Testament of Moses,' in *The Old Testament Peudepigraph*, ed. J. H. Charlesworth (New York: Doubleday, 1983), 932.

[63] A. Yarbro-Collins, 'The Composition and Redaction of the Testament of Moses,' *HTR* 69 (1976): 179–186, Priest, *ibid.*

of the heavenly temple[64]) is both a high priest with frontlet on his forehead and the angel who leads the divine army into battle against the enemies of Jerusalem.

Lines 32–33: 'and the second chief <u>watches</u> on.. Jerusale<u>m</u>' – I have translated אלוף השני as 'the second chief.' The word אלוף is generally used in the Hebrew Bible to designate the chief of Edom.[65] Here, however, the context implies that אלוף is not an enemy, but a protector who watches and defends Jerusalem. This image corresponds to the portrayal of אלפי יהודה 'the chiefs of Judea' (Zechariah 12:5–6) who destroy the enemies of Jerusalem. In the Hekhalot literature, the word אלוף serves as a title for angels.[66] Here too, I believe, the word denotes an angel, one of those who have descended on the gates of Jerusalem and Judea (lines 26–8). Hence, if one host of angels was sent to guard the cities of Judea, the second אלוף 'chief' was sent to watch over Jerusalem.

Line 35: 'that he saw a man ... works' – The text is fragmentary and difficult to understand. The word איש is followed by a gap, after which we have the word עובד. As *The Gabriel Revelation* frequently references the final chapters of Zechariah, it might be that the line reflects Zechariah 13:5 איש עובד אדמה אנכי 'I am a tiller of the land.'

Line 36: 'that a sign from Jerusalem' – The Hebrew expression is שסמן מירושלם. The word שסמן may be used to mean either סמן, סימ'ן 'a sign' (equivalent to the Greek σημεῖον) or סממן 'spice, paint.'[67] Since the word אות 'sign' appears in the following lines, it would seem that the word סמן here is synonymous. Thus, I have translated שסמן מירושלם 'that a sign from Jerusalem.'

We may assume that in an eschatological composition, 'sign' can refer to either a sign of salvation or a sign of catastrophe. The belief

---

64 S. Liebermann, *Shkiin* (Jerusalem: Wahrmann Books, 1970), 99 (Heb.); R. S. Boustan, *From Martyr to Mystic*, (Tübingen: Mohr Siebeck, 2005), 165–169.

65 See, Genesis 36:15–43; Exodus 15:15; 1. Chronicles 1:35–54.

66 See Yardeni and Elitzur, 161, n. 18.

67 See 4Q270, VI, 15. סממנים

that the signs of salvation would appear in the Temple is expressed in Josephus: 'They owed their destruction to a false prophet, who had on that day proclaimed to the people in the city that God commanded them to go up to the Temple court, to receive there signs of salvation' (*War VI.* 285).

Line 37: 'ashes and a sign of exile' – The association of ashes with mourning and exile is found in Isaiah 61:3; the prophet is sent to those who were exiled from Zion to Babylon 'to give them a garland instead of ashes.'

Line 40: <u>'That his mist will fill most of the moon'</u> – The meaning of the Hebrew למלא טחבו רוב ירח is unclear. The word טחב appears once in Rabbinic literature: אל תשתה צונן ואל תשכב בטחב meaning, we might infer from the context, 'moisture.'[68] A number of manuscripts and early prints of the Targum to Job translate the verse 37:11 אף ברי יטרח עב as ברם בטחבות יטרח עייבא.[69] Based on this reading, Kohut concluded that טחב refers to a mist or light cloud (an interpretation reinforced by the Arabic term for a light cloud, remarkably similar to טחב).[70] I have therefore translated the phrase למלא טחבו רוב ירח as <u>'That his mist will fill most of the moon'</u> – God's mist will cover a great part of the moon. Understood this way, the verse parallels Job 26:9: מאחז פני כסה פרשז עליו עננו. Several commentators interpret כסה as a reference to the full moon.[71] We may thus read both verses as dealing with the same natural phenomenon – a lunar eclipse (which takes place on full moon nights). According to Joel 2:31, one of the signs heralding 'the Day of the Lord' is the moon turning blood-red – a phenomenon which, as we know, precedes a lunar eclipse. Hence, our verse may well refer to one of the signs of salvation.

---

[68] *Sifra, Aharei Mot*, ed. Weis, 79b.
[69] See, D. M. Stec, *The Text of the Targum of Job* (Leiden: Brill, 1994), 259.
[70] A. Kohut, *Aruch Completum* 4 (Tel Aviv: Pardes, 1970), 21. See further M. Jastrow, טחבות *A Dictionary of the Targumim* (N.Y.: Hendrickson Publishers, 1975), 527.
[71] See the list of names in D. J. A. Clines, *Job 21–37, Word Biblical Commentary* (Nashville: Thomas Nelson, 2006), 622–623.

Line 41: '<u>blood</u>' – The meaning of the word is uncertain, as the first half of the line is completely illegible. If the sentence in the previous line is indeed connected to the notion of the moon turning red, we may assume that the first half of our line contained a quotation or paraphrase of the verse in Joel 2:31, ending in the word דם 'blood.'

'the <u>northerner</u> would become maggoty' – The Hebrew expression is שירם הצפוני. The word ירם may be understood as the third-person future tense of the verb רום 'rise up.' Thus, the expression שירם הצפוני may be translated as 'that the northerner would rise up,' a translation that corresponds to Joel's prophecy regarding the locust: 'I will remove the northerner [– the locust] far from you' (Joel 2:20). However, the verb ירם also appears in the Hebrew Bible in the sense of 'to putrefy;' in Exodus 16:20 we read about the manna left overnight וירם תולעים ויבאש 'and it bred worms and became foul.' This verse bears a linguistic connection to the aforementioned verse in Joel, in which the ultimate fate of 'the northerner' is described as ועלה באשו ותעל צחנתו 'the stench and foul smell of him will rise.' Assuming our author had these two verses in mind when he coined the expression שירם הצפוני, I have translated it as 'the northerner would become maggoty.'[72]

The appellation הצפוני 'the northerner' is used in the Hebrew Bible to denote an eschatological enemy who will come from the north (see Jeremiah 1:14; Ezekiel 38:6, 15). The phrase 'the northerner would become maggoty' is probably based on two prophecies: Zechariah 14:12 describes the plague with which the Lord will smite those who wage war against Jerusalem – 'their flesh will rot while they stand on their feet'; Isaiah 66:24 proclaims '[t]heir worm shall not die, their fire shall not be quenched and they become abhorrence to all flesh.' In light of these two verses, our author may well have envisioned that the northern eschatological enemy would die in a plague, his flesh breeding worms and maggots.

Line 42: '<u>abh</u>orrence the diseased spot' – The Hebrew expression is דראון הנגע. The word דראון is found in the aforementioned verse

---

[72]   See the juxtaposition of verses from Ezekiel and Haggai in lines 23–215.

in Isaiah: 'Their worm shall not die, their fire shall not be quenched and they become abhorrence [דראון] to all flesh' (66:24). Hence, our line apparently continues the description of the death of the eschatological enemy, the word הנגע 'the diseased spot' probably referring to the plague which will afflict the enemies of Jerusalem.

Line 54: '[by] three <u>days</u> this is what [I have] said' – The Hebrew verse is cut off: זה שאמ...שלשת ימין. The expression זה שאמ, it seems, ought to be read as a form of זה שאמר 'this is what I/we/you/he/they have said.' In the words שלשת ימין 'three days,' God may be reiterating His saying in line 19: לשלשת ימין תדע 'By three days you shall know.' Accordingly, I have added the letter ל before שלשת and completed the word שאמ as שאמרתי 'I have said.'

Line 56: 'please see the <u>north</u>[erner] <u>enca</u>[mps]' – The speaker asks his interlocutors to observe the northerner's encampment. As aforementioned (line 41), 'the northerner' is probably the eschatological enemy who wages war on Jerusalem. The verse also recalls the words of lines 13–14: 'now all the nations … <u>enc</u>[amp] <u>on</u> Jerusalem.' We may thus assume that the speaker is God and those asked to look at the enemy camp are the angels (just as God had previously told the angels to look for their military forces, see lines 28–29).

Line 57: 'Seal up the blood of the slaughtered of Jerusalem' – The Hebrew is סתום דם טבחי ירושל. Yardeni and Elitzur remark that the word טבחי may be interpreted as a reference to either a massacre of the people of Jerusalem or the meat of the sacrifices.[73] In this latter case, they suggest the word סתום, implying the termination of the sacrificial worship in the Temple. The subsequent reference to the blood of those slain (line 67) and to the resurrection (line 80) confirms, in my view, the first interpretation. Hence, I have translated the verse as 'the blood of the slaughtered of Jerusalem.'

    Contrary to Yardeni and Elitzur, I believe that the word סתום is to be read not as 'terminate' but as 'seal up.' We have already noted the

[73] 157, 161

strong resemblance between *The Gabriel Revelation* and Daniel 8 (see lines 20–23). In the latter text, Gabriel concluded his revelation to Daniel with the words ואתה סתם החזון כי לימים רבים 'but seal up the vision, for it pertains to many days hence,' charging the prophet to keep his words secret until the time when the vision would be fulfilled.[74] It is my opinion that the word סתום serves as yet another link between the two texts, and ought to be read in the same way in both; in *The Gabriel Revelation,* the recipient of the vision is asked to suppress his prophecy regarding those who will be slaughtered in Jerusalem. The author of the text probably understood Gabriel's words to Daniel והשחית עצומים ועם קדושים 'and he shall destroy mighty men and the people of the saints' (Daniel 8:24) as somehow related to the massacre of Jews in Jerusalem in his time, and claims this terrible event had been prophesied and kept secret for many years.

Line 60: 'He will have pity .. His mer<u>c</u>y is <u>ne</u>[ar]' – The Hebrew phrase is יחמול.. רחמו קרב (for the spelling רחמו instead of רחמיו see 2 Samuel 24:14). I have completed the phrase רחמיו קרב[ין] based on a similar expression in Aramaic רחמוי קרבין.[75] As the context would seem to suggest, the verse refers to the pity and mercy God extends toward Israel.

Line 65: 'Three holy ones of the world' – The Hebrew phrase is שלושה קדושי העולם. The word קדושים 'holy ones' is used in the Hebrew Bible and early Jewish literature to designate both angels and human beings.[76] However, the combination קדושי העולם 'holy ones of the world' seems to refer to creatures of this world only.[77] As this section of the text seems to deal with persecution and martyrdom (see the references to blood in lines 57, 67–68), the '[t]hree holy ones of the world' may be understood as 'martyrs.' The earliest composition

---

[74] See Collins, no. 54, 341–342.
[75] See *PT Taaniyot* 2:1 65a, *Pesiqta deRav Kahana*, ed. B. Mandelbaum (New York: The Jewish Theological Seminary, 1987), 283.
[76] See Collins, n. 54, 313–317.
[77] In this sense, this phrase may be compared to גדולי עולם in Rabbinic literature, also an exclusive term for humans.

to refer to martyrs as 'holy ones' is the Book of Revelation,[78] a text closely linked to *The Gabriel Revelation.*

Line 66: '<u>shalom</u> he said' – As in line 31, the word אמר 'he said' seems to serve as an introduction to human speech. The word <u>shalom</u>, in this sense, may be either part of the introduction[79] or the end of the previous, illegible verse.

'in You we tr<u>ust</u>' – The Hebrew phrase is עליך אנו בטוחין. While the human speaker is designated in the singular (אמר '<u>he</u> said'), his words seem to represent a group (אנו בטוחין '<u>we</u> trust'). Yardeni and Elitzur have noted the similarity of the phrase to a known formula in Jewish liturgy: כי על רחמיך הרבים אנו בטוחין 'Since in your great mercy we trust.'[80] Here too, the object of the profession of faith is presumably God. It is not yet clear, though, in what sense the people trust in God or what they expect Him to do.

Line 67: 'Announce him' – The Hebrew phrase is בשר לו. In the Hebrew Bible the root בשר generally expresses good tidings (the one exception being 1 Samuel 4:17).[81] We may thus interpret the verse as God's instruction to the recipient of the vision to bring good news to a third person (לו 'him') – probably the speaker of the previous line. The good tidings, in this sense, are sent in response to the speaker's declaration of faith.

'of blood, this is their chariot' – The good tidings are presumably connected to the fate of a group of people ('<u>their</u> chariot') killed by the enemies of Jerusalem. Through the recipient of the vision, God promises that the blood of the martyrs will serve as their chariot. The prophecy is probably based on the story in 2 Kings 2:11, in which Elijah goes up to heaven in a chariot of fire. I assume that the speaker

---

[78] See, ἅγιος, *Theological Dictionary of the New Testament,* Vol.1 (Grand Rapids, Michigan: Eerdmans, 1964), 110.

[79] For שלום as an introductory formula in ancient Jewish inscriptions and letters, see, Y. Sussman, 'A Halakhic Inscription from the Beth-Shean Vally,' *Tarbiz* 43 (1974): 109 (Heb.).

[80] 161, n. 19.

[81] This root bears similar meanings in other ancient Near Eastern languages. See, בשר, *Theological Dictionary of the Old Testament,* Vol. 2 (Grand Rapids, Michigan: Eerdmans, 1977), 313.

of the previous line is one of those slain, and that his words 'in you we trust' express the hope of the martyrs for ascension. However, it is equally valid to suppose that the speaker of the words of faith, who is also the subsequent recipient of the good tidings, represents the living friends or supporters of those killed.

Line 68: 'Many are those who love the Lord' – To understand this phrase we must read on to line 74. The line contains a citation of Exodus 20:6: עושה חסד לאלפים 'Showing steadfast love to thousands,' a verse which continues: לאהבי ולשמרי מצותי 'of those who love me and keep my commandments.' Our line, I believe, is a paraphrase of this part of the verse. The Rabbis understood the words לאהבי ולשמרי מצותי 'of those who love Me and keep My commandments' to mean those ready to suffer and lay down their lives for the sake of God's commandments.[82] In our context, this is most probably a reference to the aforementioned martyrs.

Line 70: 'I sent to my people my three shepherds' – The Hebrew phrase is שלחתי אל עמי שלושה רועי. This line parallels line 75: שלושה רועין יצאו לישראל 'Three shepherds went out for Israel' (with the notable difference that here the shepherds are described as רועי 'my shepherds,' sent by God to His people). The image of three shepherds is probably derived from Zechariah 11:8: ואכחד את שלשת הרעים בירח אחד 'In one month I destroyed the three shepherds.' It is unclear whether the three shepherds here share the same fate.

Line 71: 'that I have seen bless[ing]... ..... Go say(?)' – The Hebrew phrase is שראיתי. ברכ. ל..לך דבר. The second word is most probably [ה]ברכ 'blessing.' The reading 'Go say,' on the other hand, is uncertain since the original text is at this point quite indecipherable. If this is indeed the right reading, it may refer to the prophet's obligation to deliver his prophecy. The speaking voice in this line seems to be God's.

---

[82] See, *Mekilta de-Rabbi Ishmael*, Vol. 2, ed. J. Z. Lauterbach (Philadelphia: Jewish Publications Society, 1933), 247.

Line 72: 'The place <u>for</u> David the servant of the Lord' – The Hebrew is: המקום למען דוד עבד יהוה. David was mentioned in line 16 as עבדי דוד 'My servant David.' The expression (למען דוד עבדי(ו may be found in 1 Kings 11:13, 34; 2 Kings 8:19, 19:34, 20:6; Isaiah 37:35.

'The place for David' can refer to either Jerusalem or the Temple. In Rabbinic literature the word המקום 'The place' is an appellation for God.[83] While this may also serve as a plausible meaning, the unclear context and the relatively late usage of the word in this sense render such an interpretation highly unlikely.

Line 74: 'Showing steadfast love to thousands' – See line 68.

Line 75: 'Three shepherds went out for Israel' – See line 70.

Line 76: 'If there is a priest, if there are sons of holy ones' – The Hebrew phrase is אם יש כהן אם יש בני קדושים. The context is not clear. To the best of my knowledge, the precise expression בני קדושים 'sons of the holy ones' is unparalleled in ancient Hebrew literature. We do, however, have a similar expression in the Babylonian Talmud.[84] According to this tradition, Rabbi Menaham ben Simai was called בנן של קדושים 'son of the holy ones.'[85] The Talmud explains that he was awarded this epithet since he never looked at an image in his life, not even if it was stamped on a coin.[86] The meaning of the epithet in our text, though, remains uncertain, as does its possible connection to the aforementioned קדושי העולם 'holy ones of the world' (line 65).

Line 77: '<u>Who am I</u>? I am Gabriel' – This line seems to be a turning point in *The Gabriel Revelation*. Until this point, the main voice was that of God, speaking about Himself in the first person (lines 4, 12, 16–17,

---

[83] See, E. E. Urbach, *The Sages* (Jerusalem: Magnes Press,1979), 72–77.

[84] *Pesachim* 104a, *Avoda Zara* 50a.

[85] Third century CE, See, J. Florsheim, 'R. Menahem B. R. Simai,' *Tarbiz* 45 (1976): 151–153. In the Palestinian Talmud the same man is referred to as נחום איש קודש קדשים (Avoda Zara 3:1 42c).

[86] See, E. E. Urbach, *The World of the Sages* (Jerusalem: Magnes Press, 2002), 129 (Heb.); S. Schwatz, *Imperialism and Jewish Society* (Princeton: Princeton University Press, 2001), 172–173.

21, 24, 28, 31, 70, 71); God's words are directed at the recipient of the vision (lines 10, 19, 21–23, 31, 57, 67); prophetic expressions referring to the speech of God abound (lines 4, 9, 11, 13, 17–20, 29–30, 57–59, 69); and Gabriel is not mentioned explicitly (however, as we have suggested, he is probably alluded to in lines 22–23: 'the angel is supporting you'). From this point on, it is the voice of Gabriel speaking in the first person (77, 80, 83); we no longer hear the voice of God, and there are no prophetic expressions designating God's speech. Not the voice of God but rather that of Gabriel dominates the concluding section of *The Gabriel Revelation* (lines 77–87).

Line 78: 'You will rescue them' – Since the text is so fragmentary, we have no clear indication of the identity of the speaker, the addressee or those who are to be rescued.

Line 79: 'from be<u>fore</u> of you the three si[g]ns three' – The Hebrew phrase is מל<u>פניך</u> של ושה הא[ות]ן <u>ות</u> של ושה. Here too, we cannot be sure who the speaker and addressee are. We may, however, glean a certain understanding from the similar combination of מן לפניך and אות in line 17, in which God asks Ephraim (through the mediation of David) to place a sign. Analogously, this line may be read as either God or Gabriel commanding Ephraim to act concerning the 'three signs.'

Line 80: 'By three days, live' – The Hebrew phrase is לשלושת ימין חאיה. The words לשלושת ימין 'by three days' are followed by the letter ה, after which are three letters Yardeni and Elitzur claim to be undecipherable. In my opinion, the word can be clearly read as חאיה[87] (the use of the letter א as a vowel is quite common in the Hebrew Bible, the Dead Sea Scrolls and Rabbinic literature[88]).

---

[87] The letter א is completely clear (see the shape of the א of אנכי, line 77); the letter ׳ assumes different shapes throughout the text (the line underneath the ׳ here is probably only ink splatter); for the letter ה, see the appendix.

[88] On the use of the א as a vowel in 1QIsaᵃ, see E. Y. Kutscher, *The Language and Linguistic Background of the Isaiah Scroll (1QIsaᵃ)* (Leiden: Brill, 1974), 20–23; E. Qimron, *The Hebrew of the Dead Sea Scrolls* (Atlanta: Scholars Press, 1986), 21–23. Such spelling may also be found in the Hebrew Bible – see, for instance, כאביר (Isa. 10:13); וקאם (Hos. 10:14);

Gabriel, apparently, tells his interlocutor to 'live' or 'be resurrected'
(cf. Ezek. 16:6: 'In your blood, Live [חֲיִי]').

'I Gabriel <u>com</u>[mand] yo[u]' – The Hebrew phrase is אֲנִי גַבְרִיאֵל
גּוֹ[זֵר] עֲלֵי[ךָ]. The reading of the last two words is ambiguous. While
Yardeni and Elitzur read only ..ל. ..., I believe one can discern the
traces of the letters וּ after the word גַבְרִיאֵל, and the traces of the
letter עֲ before the said ל. The verb גָּזַר is used in Rabbinic literature
in connection with the performance of miracles.[89]

Line 81: 'prince of the princes' – The Hebrew phrase, שַׂר הַשָּׂרִין,
originates in Dan. 8:15–26. In his first revelation to the prophet,
Gabriel describes the 'king of bold countenance,' saying: 'and [he
shall] destroy mighty men and the people of the saints and he shall
make deceit prosper under his hand [...] and he shall even rise
up against the <u>prince of princes</u> [שַׂר שָׂרִים]' (8:24–25). This king,
Gabriel explains, is the true meaning behind the symbolic horn
Daniel had seen in a previous vision in Susa:

> It grew great, even to the host of heaven; and some of the host of
> the stars it cast down to the ground, and trampled upon them.
> It magnified itself, even up to the prince of the host; and the
> continual burnt offering was taken away from him, and the place
> of his sanctuary was overthrown. (8:10–11)

The horn that casts down the host of stars is, according to Gabriel, the
'king of bold countenance' who will defeat 'the people of the saints,'
that is – Israel. Gabriel goes on to interpret the horn's assault on the
'prince of the host' as the king's attack against the 'prince of princes.'
While the identity of this 'prince of princes' is disputed amongst
traditional commentators and modern scholars, we may surmise that

---

דְאָת (Neh. 13:16) – and the manuscripts of the Mishnah – see J. N. Epstein, *Introduction
to the Mishnaic Text* (Jerusalem: Magnes Press, 1964), 1234–1235 (Heb.). For further
discussion, see Qimron, 'Initial *Alef* as a Vowel in Hebrew and Aramaean Documents
from Qumran Compared with Other Hebrew and Aramaean Sources,' *Leshonenu* 39
(1974–75): 133–146. According to Qimron (145), this א is used primarily before or
after the letters י and ו. Prof. M. Bar Asher has suggested to me that the א of הַאִיא was
added in order to strengthen the letter ה at the beginning of the word.
[89] See *TB. Taanit*, 23a.

if the 'host of heaven' represents the People of Israel, the 'prince of the host' represents their leader. Thus, some authorities understand the 'prince of princes' to refer to the High Priest Onias III, who was murdered in Antiochia.[90] This interpretation, first offered by Ephrem Syrus, is supported by scriptural verses that label the priests as שרים 'princes' (such as שרי קדש ושרי האלהים, I Chron. 24:5)[91]. This interpretation is further corroborated by Gabriel's second revelation to Daniel, in which he foretells that 'an anointed one shall be cut off' (Dan. 9:26) – most probably referring to the assassination of Onias.[92] However, the fate of the 'prince of the host,' which the verse goes on to describe ('and the continual burnt offering was taken away from him, and the place of his sanctuary was overthrown'), might indicate that the prince is God Himself. A number of commentators adopt an intermediate position, whereby the 'prince of the host' is identified with the archangel Michael who, according to Dan. 10:21, is Israel's prince.[93] Nevertheless, for the author of *The Gabriel Revelation*, the 'prince of the princes' is probably a human leader.

Judging by the way in which it is paraphrased in our text, we may assume the author of *The Gabriel Revelation* read the prophecy in Daniel 8 as follows: the 'king of bold countenance' who 'shall make deceit prosper under his hand' (this king is presented in our text as the 'wicked branch, plastered white,' line 22) will destroy Israel – 'the people of the saints' – and attack, perhaps even kill, their leader – the 'prince of the princes.' What our text adds to the original prophecy is that Gabriel will resurrect the executed leader '[b]y three days.' Hence, it seems the author understood the 'prince of the princes' to be the earthly, rather than heavenly, leader of the People of Israel.

'the dung of the rocky crevices' – The Hebrew phrase is דומן ארובות צרים. Yardeni and Elitzur read the first word as ד..ן, yet I maintain that one can distinguish the top of a ו in the second letter, and the left part of a מ in the third,[94] thereby constructing the word דומן (dung). All the mentions of דמן in the Hebrew Bible

---

[90] On the murder of Onias, see *II Maccabees* 4:33-36.
[91] See J. A. Montgomery, *Daniel, ICC* (Edinburgh: T&T Clark, 1927), 335.
[92] See J. J. Collins, *Daniel, Hermeneia*, 356.
[93] This interpretation is suggested by Ibn Ezra. See also Collins, *Daniel*, 333.
[94] See, for instance, the shape of the מ in מן, line 83.

are connected with people who were killed but not buried, whose blood became 'as dung upon the earth.'[95] It is in this context that we should understand the depiction of the 'prince of the princes,' lying dead and unburied in 'rocky crevices,' as dung.[96]

'rocky crevices' – The Hebrew term is ארובות צרים. In biblical or Rabbinic language, ארובה means an 'opening,' 'hole' or a 'niche.' The second word I read as the deficient spelling of צורים 'rocks.'[97] ארובות צרים thus means openings or depressions in the rocks, that is – crevices. The 'rocky crevices' probably serve as the scene for the death of the 'prince of the princes.'

According to this reconstruction, Gabriel calls upon the 'prince of the princes' to come back to life: לשלושת ימין חאיה, אני גבריאל, גו[זר] על[יך] שר השרין, דומן ארובות צרים 'By three days, live, I Gabriel command you, prince of the princes, the dung of the rocky crevices.'

Line 82: 'to the <u>visions</u> (?) ... their tongue' (?) – The Hebrew is למראות ה...לשנם. The reading is uncertain, as is the translation: מראות can refer to either visions, sights or mirrors; לשנם can mean either 'their tongue' or 'their language.' Even though the combination of 'vision' and 'fire tongues' is prevalent in literature of this period,[98] the verse explicitly states 'their tongue.'

'<u>those who love me</u>' – The Hebrew word אהבי is unclear. If this is indeed the correct word, we probably ought to read it in light of line 68: אוהבין רבים ליהוה 'Many are those who love the Lord.'

Line 83: 'to me, from the three, the small one that I took, I Gabriel' – Gabriel speaks of his taking 'the small one' of the three, presumably the three shepherds mentioned in lines 70, 75. Given the

---

[95] See II Kings 9:37; Jer. 8:2; 9:21; 16:4; 25:33; Ps. 83:11.

[96] The motif of the unburied dead is common to many works similar to *The Gabriel Revelation*. Flusser (426–427, n. 51) claims this is a legendary motif based on Zech. 12:10. I, however, believe it reflects the reality of the ancient world, in which the burial of rebels was prohibited.

[97] Alternatively, one can understand צרים as enemies, but the combination ארובות צרים would then make no sense.

[98] See 1Q29 Frg. 1 l. 3 Frg. 2. line 3; 4Q376 Frg. 1ii line 1; Acts 2:3. See the discussion in J. Strugnell, 'Moses – Pseudepigrapha at Qumran,' in *Archeology and History in the Dead Sea Scrolls*, ed. L. H. Schiffman (Sheffield: JSOT Press, 1990), 240–241.

aforementioned reference to ascension (line 67), it is possible that 'took' implies the ascent to heaven (the verb לקחתי 'took' is similarly used in Genesis 5:24 to describe the ascension of Enoch: ואיננו כי לקח אתו אלהים 'and he was not, for God took him').

Line 85: 'then you will stand' – The Hebrew phrase is אז תעמדו. The identity of the speaker (Gabriel?) and addressees (the three shepherds?) is unclear. If line 83 repeated the idea of ascension mentioned in line 67, it is possible that this line reiterates the concept of resurrection mentioned in line 80 (the verb עמד 'stand' is used in the same sense in Ezekiel 37:10 and Daniel 12:13).[99]

Line 87: 'world ? /' – The mark / at the end of this and the previous line indicates the end of the composition.

---

[99] See J. F. A. Sawyer, 'Hebrew Words for the Resurrection of the Dead,' *VT* 23 (1973): 223.

Chapter 2

Structure, Themes and Historical Context

1. Structure

As noted in the preceding chapter, the opening section of *The Gabriel Revelation* is missing. We do not know for sure whether additional stones containing other parts of this composition have existed. Naturally, it is difficult to study a composition's overall structure without having access to its opening parts. We can, however, attempt to understand the structure of its readable sections.

I have stated in the commentary that the existing text of *The Gabriel Revelation* is divided into two main sections: the first ends with line 76, while lines 77–87 form the closing section. Line 77 seems to be a turning point in *The Gabriel Revelation*, where we read: מי אנכי אני גבריאל 'Who am I? I am Gabriel.' In the preceding section, the dominant speaking voice is God, Who speaks about Himself in the first person (lines 4, 12, 16–17, 21, 24, 28, 31, 70, 71). These passages contain frequent prophetic formulas that refer to God's speech (lines 4, 9, 11, 13, 17–20, 29–30, 57–59, 69). Although Gabriel is not mentioned explicitly in these passages, he is probably the angel to whom God refers in lines 22–23: 'the angel is supporting you.' In the final section there is no clear instance where God speaks in the first person. Accordingly, there are no prophetic formulas that refer to God's speech in these passages. The main voice is that of the angel Gabriel, speaking about himself in the first person (lines 77, 80, 83).

In addition to the broad division suggested above, we can further divide the surviving materials of the first part into three subsections: A. lines 9–12; B. lines 13–42; and C. lines 56–76.

A. lines 9–12

This fragmentary unit describes a dialogue between God and the vision's recipient, who hears the 'word of God' (line 9). As noted in the commentary, the references to 'asking questions' in lines 10 and 11 presumably served as an introduction to the revelation of the vision that follows. Line 12 is an introductory remark by God, Who announces that He is about to speak of 'the greatness of Jerusalem,' a phrase that probably refers to Jerusalem's miraculous salvation on the eschatological date.

B. lines 13–42

This section describes Jerusalem's salvation at the end of the eschatological war. In lines 13–16 we read about the gentile nations encamping around Jerusalem and of the groups exiled from the city. Lines 16–17 present the request from Ephraim to place the sign, probably portending the coming redemption, which is also announced by God's statement that His 'gardens' are ripe and ready for Israel (lines 18–19). This is followed by another announcement referring to the breaking of evil and the 'evil branch' within three days (lines 19–22). Then, the vision's recipient is encouraged in preparation of the imminent arrival of God's glory that will shake the heaven and the earth (lines 22–26). God is accompanied by the angels who descend in seven chariots to the gates of Judea and Jerusalem (lines 25–31). At the end of line 31 we see the frontlet, which, as we have suggested, probably belongs to Michael, leader of the angelic army. The following lines of this section, 32–42, are very fragmentary: In lines 32–33 we see the 'chief' who guards Jerusalem. The prominent element in lines 36–40 is the motif of the 'signs.' The last two lines of this section, 41–42, were probably devoted to the description of the plague that would afflict the enemy during the eschatological war. (The following lines, 43–55, are too fragmentary to allow determination of their contents).

C. Lines 56–76

The people killed before the time of salvation comprise the main theme of this unit. It thus precedes chronologically the earlier section devoted mainly to the redemptive event. There are also, however, some significant points of similarity between the two sections. They share an almost identical opening, both beginning with a reference to the enemy encampment (line 56 which parallels lines 13–4). In the previous section, this reference was followed by the request from Ephraim to place the 'sign' (lines 16–17). Here it is followed by a reference to the blood of those slaughtered in Jerusalem. Is it possible to infer from this that Ephraim's 'sign' is connected to the blood of those slain by the enemy?

The text that follows the prophetic formula in lines 57–59 is very fragmentary until line 65, in which the three 'holy ones of the world' are mentioned. Line 66 presents the statement of those who trust 'you,' probably a reference to God. In reply, God orders the vision's recipient to 'announce him of blood, this is their chariot' (line 67). This is followed by the statement about the many who love God (line 68). As noted in the commentary, this statement echoes Exodus 20:6, quoted partially later in line 74. Between lines 68 and 74, we find God's reference to the three shepherds He has sent to Israel (line 70); this statement is repeated slightly differently in line 75. The section ends with the statement about the priest and the 'sons of the holy ones,' which is probably related in some way to the reference to the 'three holy ones of the world' in line 65.

In the small sub-unit of lines 65–76 then, we find three instances of internal references between different lines: 65 and 76, 68 and 74, 70 and 75.

The final section of *The Gabriel Revelation* (lines 77–87) is fragmentary. As noted above, the main speaking voice is that of the angel Gabriel, who speaks about himself in the first person (lines 77, 80, 83). The main themes of the readable words of this section seem to pertain to the resurrection and ascension. The resurrection of the 'prince of the princes' is described in lines 80–81, followed by Gabriel's statement about the 'small one' that he took (line 83). This act probably refers to taking the 'small one' to heaven, i.e. his ascension. Finally, we encounter the statement 'then you will stand' (line 85), which probably refers to the resurrection of unidentified individuals. In light of the many points of similarity between *The Gabriel Revelation* and the book of Daniel, we can compare this ending to the concluding chapter in Daniel, which contains references to resurrection (Daniel 12:2, 13) and ascension (12:3). The similarity increases if we accept the common view[1] that the 'man clothed in linen,' who is the main speaker in Daniel 12, is the angel Gabriel. We find, therefore, that the two compositions end with a speech by Gabriel referring to resurrection and ascension.

2. Who is the recipient of the vision?

In the first part of *The Gabriel Revelation*, God directs his speech several times to a person who seems to be the recipient of the vision (lines 10, 19, 21–23, 31, 57, 67). This person is invited to ask God about the 'evil branch' (line 21), receives words of encouragement (lines 22–23), is asked about the frontlet (line 31) and is instructed to 'conceal the blood' and announce the blood that turns into a chariot (lines 57, 67). However, the surviving text lacks any clear statement regarding the identity of this vision's recipient.

The words of encouragement in lines 22–23 'the angel is supporting you. Do not fear,' seem to indicate that they are addressed to a human being who is supported by an angel. As noted in the commentary on these lines, the entire scene is based on Daniel 8:16–18, Gabriel's revelation before Daniel. We may note at this juncture the other points of similarity found between this revelation and *The Gabriel Revelation* (see the commentary to lines 20, 57, 82 and the above discussion of the ending of the two compositions). Can we infer from this similarity that the recipient of the vision in *The Gabriel Revelation* is the biblical Daniel? This is quite plausible. At the same time, there are also significant differences that need to be taken into account: The biblical Daniel has visions and dreams in which the angel Gabriel addresses him, but Daniel does not hear God's direct speech like

---

[1]   See J. J. Collins, *Daniel, Hermeneia,* 373.

the prophets preceding him. In contrast, in *The Gabriel Revelation* God speaks directly to the vision's recipient and frequent prophetic references to God's speech appear styled after earlier prophetic books. Thus, *The Gabriel Revelation* demonstrates an attempt to imitate the revelatory style of classical prophesy rather than that of the book of Daniel. In this respect, *The Gabriel Revelation* clearly differs from the pseudo-Daniel compositions from Qumran, in which an obvious attempt to imitate the style of Daniel is evident.[2]

Another possible solution to the enigmatic identity of the vision's recipient emerges from a comparison between the first and the last parts of *The Gabriel Revelation*. The concluding section contains three instances of speech in the second person singular. In two of these cases (תצילם 'rescue them' line 78 and מלפניך 'from before of you' line 79) both the speaker's and the recipient's identity is unknown. The third instance is the instruction לשלושת ימין חאיה 'by three days, live,' uttered by Gabriel (line 80). According to our reconstruction, the recipient of this instruction is the person who is called שר השרין 'prince of the princes.' In one of God's speeches to the vision's recipient in the first part, we find a statement that opens with the same words as Gabriel's instruction: לשלשת ימין תדע 'by three days you will know' (line 19). One may assume that these similar statements are addressed to the same person. Initially this person is told by God that in three days he will learn that 'the evil has been broken by righteousness.' Later on, he is instructed by Gabriel to resurrect in three days. Thus, the day of his resurrection will coincide with the day of the breaking of evil. Following this line of thought, we may conclude that the vision's recipient is the same person resurrected by Gabriel, i.e. the 'prince of the princes' who has the vision after his death, but prior to his resurrection. While this reading is plausible, other tenable options remain: We can still maintain that the day of the resurrection will coincide with the day of the breaking of evil, but can claim that the announcement about the breaking of the evil was not relayed to the resurrected individual but to someone else. Ultimately, the poor preservation of the text prevents us from ascertaining the identity of the recipient of the vision in *The Gabriel Revelation*.

[2] 4Q243–245

3. Biblical Context and Ideology

As we have seen in the commentary, the text contains many allusions to the final chapters of the book of Zechariah. It seems that the construction of the section between lines 13–42 is largely based on Zechariah 14. In lines 13–16 we read about the gentiles who encamp around Jerusalem and the groups of people exiled from the city. This scene is based on Zechariah 14:2:

> For I will gather all the nations against Jerusalem to battle, and the city shall be taken and the houses plundered and the women ravished; half of the city shall go into exile, but the rest of the people shall not be cut off from the city.

Lines 24–31 describe the appearance of God, Who shakes the earth, and the angels descending in chariots. This scene is mainly based on Zechariah 14:3–5:

> Then the Lord will go forth and fight against those nations as when he fights on a day of battle. On that day his feet shall stand on the Mount of Olives which lies before Jerusalem on the east; and the Mount of Olives shall be split in two from east to west by a very wide valley; so that one half of the Mount shall withdraw northward, and the other half southward.

> And the valley of my mountains shall be stopped up, for the valley of the mountains shall touch the side of it; and you shall flee as you fled from the earthquake in the days of Uzziah king of Judah. Then the Lord your God will come and all the holy ones with him.

The 'holy ones' who will accompany God are the angels, which, according to *The Gabriel Revelation*, will descend in their chariots.

Finally, we have the fragmentary lines 41–42. The readable words in these lines testify that the main subject here is the plague God will inflict upon the nations:

And this shall be the plague with which the LORD will smite all the peoples that wage war against Jerusalem: their flesh shall rot while they are still on their feet, their eyes shall rot in their sockets, and their tongues shall rot in their mouths (Zechariah 14:12).

Other possible allusions to Zechariah are to be found in line 32 (אלוף 'chief' see Zech. 12:6), line 35 (עובד...איש see Zech. 13:5) and in lines 70, 75 (שלושה רועין 'the three shepherds' see Zech. 11:8).

The other biblical text figuring prominently in this composition is the book of Daniel. We have already pointed at the similarity between the conclusions of the two compositions. A particularly strong link between *The Gabriel Revelation* and Gabriel's revelation to Daniel is evident in Daniel 8:16–27. As noted above, the words of encouragement in lines 22–23 'the angel is supporting you. Do not fear' echo Daniel 8:17–18 in the depiction of the revelation scene:

> So he came near where I stood; and when he came, I was frightened and fell upon my face... As he was speaking to me, I fell into a deep sleep with my face to the ground; but he touched me and set me on my feet.

The figure of the 'evil branch' in lines 21–22 is probably connected to the figure of the 'king of bold countenance' in Daniel 8:23. The announcement about the breaking of evil in lines 20–21 mirrors the announcement about the breaking of the 'king of bold countenance' in Daniel 8:25. The instruction to 'seal up' סתום in line 57 probably echoes the similar instruction in Daniel 8:26. And finally, the reference to שר השרין 'prince of the princes' clearly relies on the שר שרים 'prince of princes' in Daniel 8:25.

According to our reconstruction and reading of the text of *The Gabriel Revelation*, this 'prince of the princes' is the leader of Israel resurrected by the angel Gabriel. The notion of the death of the 'prince of the princes' is probably based on Daniel 8:25: 'and he shall even rise up against the Prince of princes.' However, the author of *The Gabriel Revelation* may have also relied at this point on the angel Gabriel's statement in his second revelation to Daniel: 'And after the sixty-two weeks, an anointed one shall be cut off' (Daniel 9:26).

Jerome has noted that the Jews understood this verse as a reference to the death of the messiah.[3] C. C. Torrey went as far as claiming that this verse indeed referred to the death of the Messiah son of Ephraim.[4] I accept the common view that originally the verse referred to the death of Onias III. However, in light of the reference in line 16 of *The Gabriel Revelation* to a messianic figure, 'Ephraim,' and the close relation of this composition to the scriptural account of the revelation of Gabriel to Daniel, it is possible that the author of this composition understood the verse in Daniel 9:26 to bear similar meaning to that suggested by Torrey. While it is true that in the surviving materials of *The Gabriel Revelation* there is no clear reference to Daniel 9:24–27, such references might exist in the missing parts.

It seems that the author of *The Gabriel Revelation* used his interpretation of the scriptures of Daniel to develop a notion of Catastrophic Messianism.[5] He probably read the verses in the book of Daniel to mean the following: The 'king of bold countenance' will fight against the people of Israel who are 'the people of the saints' of Daniel 8:24; and as this verse states, he will destroy and kill many of them. As this catastrophe will unfold, a leader of Israel, 'the prince of princes,' will be killed as Daniel 8:25 states. The author might also have based the notion of the messianic leader's death on the verse 'And after the sixty-two weeks, an anointed one shall be cut off' (Daniel 9:26). The final salvation would arrive only after all these calamities when the evil king would be miraculously smitten 'but, by no human hand, he shall be broken' (Daniel 8:25). Thus, according to this reading of the scriptures, the death of the leader, the 'prince of princes,' is an essential part of the redemptive process and the final event preceding the miraculous annihilation of the evil king!

Three is the most frequently mentioned number in *The Gabriel Revelation*. The phrase ימין לשלשת 'by three days' appears three times in the surviving materials and possesses unique significance. The first appearance, in line 19, introduces the announcement of the breaking of evil. The second (line 54) is part of a fragmentary

[3]   See J. Braverman, *Jerome's Commentary on Daniel* (Washington: Baker Book House, 1978), 106–107.
[4]   'The Messiah Son of Ephraim,' *JBL* 66 (1947): 268–272.
[5]   See G. Scholem, *The Messianic Idea in Judaism* (New York: Schoken, 1971), 8–18.

sentence. The third appearance (line 80) is part of Gabriel's instruction of resurrection. The phrase לשלשת ימין 'by three days' is not to be found in the above-mentioned chapters of Zechariah and Daniel. The 'third day' appears in a redemptive context in the metaphorical resurrection of Hosea 6:1–2:

> Come, let us return to the Lord; for he has torn, that he may heal us;
> he has stricken, and he will bind us up.
> After two days he will revive us;
> on the third day he will raise us up,
> that we may live before him.

That this verse supports Gabriel's instruction 'By three days, live' is quite clear. It is also possible that the announcement of the breaking of evil 'by three days' is based on these scriptures. As noted above, the final salvation will come in the wake of major catastrophes. The words of Hosea, '… for he has torn, that he may heal us; he has stricken, and he will bind us up. After two days he will revive us; on the third day he will raise us up,' match well the salvation that follows the devastating destruction wreaked by the onslaught of the evil forces.

Another prophetic book that influenced *The Gabriel Revelation* is the book of Joel. The reference to the enemy as 'the northerner' in lines 41 and 56 is based on Joel 2:20. An implicit reference to this book also appears in line 67 בשר לו על דם זו המרכבה שלהן 'announce him of blood, this is their chariot.' The use of the indefinite form for דם 'blood' seems odd, as the definite form, הדם '*the* blood', would have been more appropriate. The use of the word זו 'this' in this context is also peculiar. The notion of the blood's transformation into a chariot for the slain people could have been expressed more simply with, for example, a formulation like יהי/היהפוך למרכבה שלהן הדם 'the blood will be / will become their chariot.'

I wish to suggest that this passage might contain a concealed *midrash* or *pesher* to the above-mentioned verses of Joel 3:3–4 (English 2:30–31): ונתתי מופתים בשמים ובארץ דם ואש ותמרות עשן, השמש יהפך לחשך והירח לדם לפני בוא יום ה' הגדול והנורא

And I will give portents in the heavens and on the earth, <u>blood</u> and fire and columns of smoke. The sun shall be turned to darkness, and the moon to <u>blood</u>, before the great and terrible day of the Lord comes.

The phrase דם זו המרכבה שלהן 'Blood is their chariot' could be read as a midrashic interpretation of the word דם 'blood' appearing in the first verse: According to this verse, God 'will give portents in the heavens and on the earth, blood...' The author of *The Gabriel Revelation* asserts that the blood appearing in the heavens and on the earth is the blood of the slain people who will ascend to heaven from the earth. We may thus identify this passage as a typical midrashic saying – a quotation of a biblical verse followed by its interpretation: 'דם' – זו המרכבה שלהן 'blood' means their chariot.' While *The Gabriel Revelation* predates the golden age of the Rabbinic era, sages were already active in the Herodian period and the midrashic mode of interpretation was known.[6]

The suggested association between the blood of the slain people and the passages from Joel about the portents of the coming of the Day of the Lord can be supported by two other apocalyptic texts. The first is the *Testament of Moses* (TM). While scholars disagree on its genesis,[7] there seems to be a wide consensus that the present version of TM was composed circa the early first century CE,[8] i.e. in the same period of *The Gabriel Revelation*'s inscription. In the ninth chapter of TM we read about Taxo, who tells his sons they should die rather than

---

[6] On Midrashic activity in the Herodian period see J. N. Epstein, *Introduction to Tannaitic*, (Jerusalem: Magnes Press, 1957), 510–512 (Heb.); M. I. Kahana, 'The Halakhic Midrashim,' in *The Literature of the Sages, Second Part*, eds. S. Safrai, et al. (Amsterdam: Fortress Press, 2006), 13–15.

[7] On the debate about a possible Antiochan date for the main part of the book see, J. J. Collins, 'The Date and Provenance of the Testament of Moses,' in *Studies on the Testament of Moses*, ed. G. W. E. Nickelsburg Jr (Cambridge MA: Society of Biblical Literature,1973), 15–32; G. W. E. Nickelsburg Jr, 'An Antiochan Date for the Testament of Moses,' *ibid.*, 33–37; J. J. Collins, 'Some Remaining Traditio-Historical Problems,' *ibid.*, 38–43; J. Priest, 'Testament of Moses' in *The Old Testament Pseudepigrapha*, ed. J. H. Charlesworth (New York: Doubleday, 1983), 920–921; J. Tromp, *The Assumption of Moses: A Critical Edition with Commentary*, SVTP 10 (Leiden: Brill, 1993), 115–121; K. Atkinson, 'Taxo Martyrdom and the Role of the *Nuntius* in the Testament of Moses,' *JBL* 125 (2006): 457–467.

[8] See, R. H. Charles, *The Assumption of Moses* (London: Clarendon Press, 1897), lv–lviii; Atkinson, *ibid.*, 467.

transgress the commandments of the Lord, 'For if we do this, and do die, our blood will be avenged before the Lord.'[9] This is immediately followed by the description of the arrival of the eschatological war and salvation. J. Licht[10] had pointed out the significance of the linkage between Taxo's blood and the vengeance. According to his interpretation, 'the sense of Taxo's speech and the virtue of his deed appear to be this: God cannot allow innocent blood to be shed unavenged. Let us therefore die innocently, and we shall thus surely promote Divine vengeance and deliverance.'[11]

In the description of the signs of the eschatological time, we read the following:

The sun will not give light.
And in darkness the horns of the moon will flee.
Yea, they will be broken in pieces.
It will be turned wholly into blood.[12]

This description is clearly based on the verses in Joel.[13] In the unique context of TM we can see the link between the blood of Taxo and his sons, which will be avenged by God, and the transformation of the moon into blood. Thus, the sanguine moon attests to the shedding of Taxo's blood and for this reason provides a sign for the impending day of vengeance.

Similar ties can be found in the book of Revelation (6:9–12, 15–17):

When he opened the fifth seal, I saw under the altar the souls of those who had been slain for the word of God and for the witness they had borne; they cried out with a loud voice, 'O Sovereign

---

[9] TM 9:7; J. Priest, 'Testament of Moses,' 931.
[10] J. Licht, 'Taxo, or the Apocalyptic Doctrine of vengeance,' *JJS* 12 (1961): 96–100.
[11] Licht, *ibid.*, 97. Priest (923) claims that the association between the blood and the vengeance does not prove that Taxo intended 'to compel God to exercise His vengeance' as Licht (98) had argued. However, see J. J.Collins, *The Apocalyptic Imagination* (Grand Rapids: Eerdmans, 1998), 131.
[12] TM 10:5, J. Priest, 932.
[13] See R. H. Charles, 'The Assumption of Moses' in *The Apocrypha and Pseudepigrapha of the Old Testament*, Vol 2. ed. R. H. Charles (Oxford: Clarendon Press, 1913), 422.

Lord, holy and true, how long before thou wilt judge and avenge our blood on those who dwell upon the earth?' Then they were each given a white robe and told to rest a little longer, until the number of their fellow servants and their brethren should be complete, who were to be killed as they themselves had been.

When he opened the sixth seal, I looked, and behold, there was a great earthquake; and the sun became black as sackcloth, the full moon became like blood... Then the kings of the earth and the great men and the generals and the rich and the strong, and every one, slave and free, hid in the caves and among the rocks of the mountains, calling to the mountains and rocks, 'Fall on us and hide us from the face of him who is seated on the throne, and from the wrath of the Lamb; for the great day of their wrath has come, and who can stand before it?'

A clear link is evident between the blood of 'those who had been slain for the word of God and for the witness they had borne' and the coming of 'the great day of wrath.' When there is 'sufficient' blood, the moon turns sanguine and becomes a sign for the approach of 'the great day of wrath.'

Thus, it seems that both in TM and in Revelation the blood of the slain is reflected in the color of the moon, which signifies the day of the Lord on which He will inflict His vengeance.

This link sheds light on the relationship between the two appearances of chariots in *The Gabriel Revelation*: The descending chariots of the angels in line 26 and the ascending chariot with the blood of the slain in line 67. The blood in a chariot ascending before the Lord in heaven announces the coming of the day of the Lord, when God will descend with His angels from heaven. On that day, the angels will descend in the chariots on the gates of Judea and Jerusalem and take vengeance on the culprits for the blood of the slain.

Earlier in this chapter, the discussion of *The Gabriel Revelation*'s structure raised the possibility that the 'sign' of Ephraim is connected to the blood of those slain by the enemy. The present discussion seems to affirm this assumption. It appears that as in TM and Revelation, here also, the blood of the victims of the carnage serves as the sign of and cause for the coming of revenge and salvation.

This leads us to examine the biblical context of the figure of 'Ephraim' in *The Gabriel Revelation*. I have pointed out in the first chapter the scriptures of Hosea (11:1–9) and Jeremiah (31:9, 18–20) as sources for considering Ephraim as God's firstborn, His tormented and beloved son. Hosea says: 'Yet it was I who taught Ephraim to walk …How can I give you up, Oh Ephraim …My heart recoils within me, my compassion grows warm and tender.' Jeremiah develops this image of Ephraim:

> … I am a father to Israel,
> and Ephraim is my first-born…
> I have heard Ephraim bemoaning,
> 'Thou hast chastened me, and I was chastened,
> like an untrained calf;
> bring me back that I may be restored,
> for Thou art the Lord my God.
> For after I had turned away I repented;
> and after I was instructed, I smote upon my thigh;
> I was ashamed, and I was confounded,
> because I bore the disgrace of my youth.'
> Is Ephraim my dear son?
> Is he my darling child?
> For as often as I speak against him,
> I do remember him still.
> Therefore my heart yearns for him;
> I will surely have mercy on him, says the Lord.

However, we also find a different portrait of Ephraim, the image of the mighty warrior: 'Then Ephraim shall become like a mighty warrior' (Zechariah 10:7). This image is related to the depiction of Joseph, Ephraim's father, as a mighty bull or wild ox:

> His firstling bull has majesty,
> and his horns are the horns of the wild ox,
> with them he shall push the peoples,
> all of them, to the ends of the earth,
> such are the ten thousands of Ephraim.
>
> (Deuteronomy 33:17)

By merging these two biblical images of Ephraim, we arrive at a figure of a mighty warrior possessing the messianic titles of God's firstborn and beloved son. Ephraim the mighty warrior is also a suffering and afflicted son of God.

J. Heinemann has argued that the original image of Ephraim as messiah was that of a mighty warrior, and that only Bar Kokhba's defeat in 135 CE generated the motif of the death of this messiah.[14] It seems, however, that the discovery of *The Gabriel Revelation* indicates otherwise. In lines 16–18 we read the following:

> My servant David,
> ask of Ephraim
> [that he p]lace the sign;
> (this) I ask of you.
> For thus said the Lord of Hosts, the God of Israel,
> My gardens are ripe
> My holy thing for Israel

God requests of his servant David to approach Ephraim and ask him to place the 'sign' due to the ripening of His gardens.

This is an astonishing scene: David functions here as a servant who is sent by his master, God, to ask Ephraim to place the 'sign.' In the context of the following lines of *The Gabriel Revelation* (18–19), it appears that since God's gardens are ripe, there is an urgent need for Ephraim to place the 'sign.' Ephraim seems to enjoy a higher status than David. The servant David is only a messenger sent to Ephraim, while the latter, rather than David, is entrusted with the performance of the decisive act.

As mentioned in the commentary, God's gardens seem to be the Kingdom of Heaven. God's gardens are ready and ripe for Israel; the redemptive process must begin, but the necessary trigger is Ephraim's placement of the 'sign.' As noted above, Ephraim's 'sign' is probably related to the blood of those slain by the enemy. In light of the image of the biblical Ephraim as a mighty warrior who is also the suffering

---

[14] See J. Heineman, 'The Messiah of Ephraim and the Premature Exodus of the Tribe of Ephraim,' *HTR* 68 (1975): 1–15.

son of God, I would like to suggest a more precise understanding of this sign. It is possible that Ephraim of *The Gabriel Revelation* is the heavenly image of the 'prince of the princes' who is later to be resurrected by Gabriel. The 'prince of princes' in *The Gabriel Revelation* is an earthly leader of Israel, probably a messianic leader, who was killed by the enemy. This slain leader conforms to a high degree with the image of biblical Ephraim, a warrior, suffering son of God. If this understanding of 'Ephraim' is true, then Ephraim's 'sign' can be understood to be his own blood. It is only after this messianic leader is killed and his blood is placed as a sign that the process of salvation can begin. This understanding accords very well with the ideology of Catastrophic Messianism that, as we have suggested above, is reflected in *The Gabriel Revelation* by the use of the scriptures of Daniel.

Thus, 'Ephraim's' role in the redemptive process is similar to that of Taxo. Both place the sign of blood before God and in this way promote the coming of the day of vengeance and salvation. J. Licht explored the tension between the deterministic view of history reflected in TM (where the future events are already predicted by Moses) and the fact that 'Taxo is expected to influence history in its most decisive point.'[15] I believe that we have a similar case in *The Gabriel Revelation*: The coming of salvation is predicted by God in His speech to the recipient of the vision. Yet the entire process seems to depend on Ephraim who must place the sign! This may explain God's pleading tone when addressing Ephraim: He does not command Ephraim to place the sign but rather sends His servant David to request (בקש) that Ephraim place it.

4. Date and Provenance

As noted above, Ada Yardeni has dated the script of *The Gabriel Revelation* to the late the first century BCE or the early first century CE.[16] This estimate provides us only with the latest possible date for the

---

[15] Licht, 'Taxo, or the Apocalyptic Doctrine of Vengeance,' 99.
[16] A. Yardeni and B. Elitzur, 'Document: A First-Century BCE Prophetic Text Written on a Stone: First Publication,' *Cathedra* 123 (2007): 162–166.

composition of *The Gabriel Revelation*, since the surviving inscription may have been copied from an earlier text. However, Yardeni and Elitzur also determine, based on the text's language, that it was composed 'around the end of the first century BCE.'[17] Hence, we may assume that *The Gabriel Revelation* was composed and written around the turn of the Common Era.

There are indications that *The Gabriel Revelation* was written against the backdrop of a military conflict. The mention of 'the slaughtered of Jerusalem' and of 'the nations who encamp around Jerusalem' might refer to a bloody event instigated by gentiles in Jerusalem. In fact, in the late first century BCE a gentile army was indeed responsible for a massive bloodshed in both Jerusalem and throughout the country: the rebellion that broke out in April, 4 BCE, following the death of King Herod the Great. The insurgents sought to free themselves from the yoke of the Roman-supported Herodian line. The insurrection began in Jerusalem and spread throughout the province. It was finally crushed by the Roman army under the command of Varus, Governor of Syria. Thousands were killed or sold to slavery and parts of the Temple were burnt.[18]

Josephus tells us that this revolt was led by three men, all of whom possessed aspirations to the throne,[19] i.e. the three had messianic pretensions.[20] *The Gabriel Revelation* mentions the 'three shepherds' who were sent to Israel (see lines 70, 75). Since the Hebrew רועה 'shepherd' might refer to a king or messianic leader,[21] it is possible that the 'three shepherds' are the three messianic leaders of this

[17] *Ibid.*,156.
[18] See Josephus, *B.J.* 2:1-5; *Ant* 17:10 (250–298); TM 6:8-9.
[19] On the leaders of the revolt, see W. R. Farmer, 'Judas, Simon and Athrogenes,' *NTS* 4 (1958:) 147–55; M. Stern, 'Herod and the Herodian Dynasty,' in *The Jewish People in the First Century*, eds. S. Safrai and M. Stern (Assen: Van Gorcum, 1974), 280; R. H. Horsley, *Bandits, Prophets and Messiahs* (Harrisburg, PA: Continuum International Publishing Group, 1999), 111–117; Nikos Kokkinos, 'The Herodian Dynasty,' *Journal for the Study of the Pseudoepigrapha Supplement Studies 30* (1998): 227, n. 79.
[20] See, M. Stern, 'Herod and the Herodian Dynasty,' in *The Jewish People in the First Century*, ed. S. Safrai and M. Stern (Assen: Van Gorcum, 1974), 280; M. Hengel, *The Zealots*, trans. D. Smith (Edinburgh: T&T Clark, 1989), 292, 328–329; Horsley, *Bandits, Prophets and Messiahs*, 114–117; Horsley, 'Popular Messianic Movement around the Time of Jesus', *CBQ* 46 (1984): 484–487. See also the more skeptical view of M. Goodman, *The Ruling Class in Judea*, (Cambridge: Cambridge University Press, 1995), 92.
[21] See Jeremiah 3:15, 23:1; Ezekiel 34:2–23. One of the three leaders of the revolt, Athronges, was a shepherd by vocation.

rebellion. While at the time of the rebellion each of these leaders had one group of supporters, after the rebellion they could be seen as one unit of 'three shepherds,' similar to the three shepherds mentioned in the book of Zechariah (11:8).

As mentioned in the commentary, the text reconstruction of the poorly preserved line, (line 40) 'That his mist will fill most of the moon,' might refer to a lunar eclipse. In light of our previous discussion of the blood of the slain as a sign also appearing in the sanguine moon, we may consider line 67 to contain another covert reference to a lunar eclipse: 'Announce him of blood, this is their chariot.' The blood of the slain ascends to heaven and, as written in the scriptures of the book of Joel, also appears on the bloody moon. Since the moon assumes a sanguine appearance before its eclipse, it is possible that these lines reflect an event that claimed many lives shortly prior to a lunar eclipse. Such an event indeed took place soon before the outbreak of the revolt of 4 BCE.

Not long before Herod's death, two sages, Judas and Matthias, encouraged their disciples to pull down the golden eagle that was fixed by King Herod above the Temple gate. Judas, Matthias and their disciples were captured after removing the eagle. They were brought before Herod, who sentenced some forty of them to death.[22] Josephus further remarks: 'And on that same night there was an eclipse of the moon.'[23] Most scholars agree that the reference is to the lunar eclipse that occurred on 13 March, 4 BCE.[24] The revolt began a month later, during Passover. It is therefore possible that the reference to the lunar eclipse in line 40 and the mention of the blood that turns into a chariot in line 67 reflect this event. The sanguine moon on the night of 13 March, 4 BCE was probably taken as a sign that the righteous people who gave their life for pulling down the effigy from

---

[22] See Josephus, *B.J.* 1:648–655; *Ant* 17 (151–167).

[23] *Ant* 17 (167).

[24] See the discussion and literature in D. R. Schwartz, *Studies in the Jewish Background of Christianity* (Tübingen: Mohr Siebeck, 1992), 157–8. I cannot accept his suggestion (*ibid.*, 161) that the lunar eclipse mentioned by Josephus occurred not on the night of the execution, but rather 'on the night Matthias ben Theophilus dreamed his fateful dream.' The syntax and structure of Josephus' story clearly point to the fact that the notion of the lunar eclipse is connected to the burning of the 'other Matthias' mentioned in the previous sentence, and not to the story about the dream of Matthias ben Theophilus that was told earlier.

the temple gate had ascended to heaven and were seen on the moon. A. Yarbro Collins has suggested[25] that TM 10:8–9 is an allusion to the pulling down of the golden eagle. It is thus possible that these two apocalyptic compositions, compiled around the same time, referred to this event.

Finally, we should examine the possible identification of the 'prince of the princes' resurrected by Gabriel. As noted in the commentary, it seems that this person was an earthly leader of Israel. The Jewish and Roman sources tell us about Simon of Transjordan who was probably the prominent among the three leaders of the revolt.[26] He proclaimed himself king and was seen as such by his supporters, who undoubtedly viewed him as the fulfilment of their messianic hopes. Josephus describes Simon's death after being defeated on the battlefield:

> Simon himself, endeavouring to escape up a steep ravine, was intercepted by Gratus [Herod's military commander], who struck the fugitive from the side a blow on the neck, which severed his head from his body.[27]

According to the account in *The Gabriel Revelation*, the 'prince of princes' became as 'dung in the rocky crevices' after his death. Thus, the mention of the 'rocky crevices' close to that of the death of the 'prince of princes' might allude to the killing of Simon – the leader of the revolt who had assumed the mantle of royalty – in the rocky crevices of Transjordan.

It is thus possible that *The Gabriel Revelation* was composed shortly after 4 BCE, against the backdrop of the crushing of the revolt.

Our understanding of the possible historical context of *The Gabriel Revelation* may shed light on the aim and orientation of this

---

25 'The Composition and Redaction of the Testament of Moses,' *HTR* 69 (1976): 186. See further, J. J. Collins, 'The Testament (Assumption) of Moses,' in *Outside the Old Testament*, ed. M. de Jonge (Cambridge: Cambridge University Press, 1985), 148, 157.

26 Simon's prominent role among the leaders of the rebellion is evident in that he is the only one mentioned by the Roman historian Tacitus (*Histories* 5:9:2), who also states that Simon crowned himself as king. See further, M. Smallwood, *The Jews Under Roman Rule* (Leiden: Brill, 1972), 111, n. 26.

27 Josephus. War 2:4:2, trans. H. St. J. Thackeray, *LCL*, 345

composition, as well as on the conditions that led to its inscription on the stone. I assume that this text was composed and written within a group of followers of the messianic leader Simon, who was killed in Transjordan in 4 BCE. The stone was probably found in an area across in Jordan, near the eastern shore of the Dead Sea.[28] As noted in the introduction,[29] it is possible that it was placed as a memorial. Hence, we may suggest the possibility that it was installed in the ground not far from the site of Simon's death in his commemoration.

The text of *The Gabriel Revelation* possibly reflects the struggle of the members of this group with the crisis that followed the killing of their messianic leader and the merciless crushing of the rebellion by the Roman army. Such an event would naturally lead the followers of the slain leader to question his messianic pretensions and take his death as evidence that he was a false messiah: The author of *The Gabriel Revelation*, however, disqualifies such a view as he shapes the ideology of Catastrophic Messianism based on Gabriel's address to Daniel. According to this ideology, the defeat and death of the messianic leader is an essential part of the redemptive process. The blood of the slain messiah, who will be resurrected within three days, paves the way for the final salvation.

The author of *The Gabriel Revelation* exhibits well-developed apocalyptic thinking. He speaks in the name of God and also uses the Tetragramaton frequently. He also mentions prophets as an existing reality (line 15). It is thus difficult to believe that the author was a Pharisee. At the same time, his style is different from that of the Qumran community and there are no indications of Qumranic concepts or terms in this composition. Further, the reference to 'Ephraim' as a positive and significant figure in *The Gabriel Revelation* contradicts the use of 'Ephraim' in the Dead Sea Scrolls as a negative title for the Pharisees.[30] The author's political views and his belief in resurrection indicate that he is definitely not a Sadducee either. If

---

[28] See Introduction, xi.
[29] See xiv.
[30] See D. Flusser, 'Pharisees, Sadducees and Essenes in Pesher Nahum,' *Essays in Jewish History and Philology in Memory of Gedaliahu Alon*, eds. M. Dorman et al (Tel Aviv: Dvir, 1970), 133–168.

The Gabriel Revelation was indeed written shortly after 4 BCE, then it predates the time of the formation of the 'fourth philosophy' of the zealots.[31] Hence, we cannot attribute this composition to any known Jewish sect of the period.

We can, however, point to another composition redacted in the same period, which shares many of the views of *The Gabriel Revelation* and probably belongs to similar apocalyptic circles: the Testament of Moses (TM). These two compositions share a similar understanding of their time. Immediately after the description of the cruel crushing of the revolt in TM 6:8–9, we find the following remark: 'When this has taken place, the times will quickly come to an end.'[32] As Atkinson notes:[33] 'The author apparently believed that the partial destruction of the temple and the other tumultuous events that followed Herod the Great's death were signs that signalled the beginning of the final age of History.' I believe that these exact same words can be applied to the author of *The Gabriel Revelation*.

In the final part of TM 7:1, we read: 'The four hours shall come.'[34] J. J. Collins has noted that the 'four hours' in TM 7:1 are probably an apocalyptic formulation based on Daniel 7:25. He suggests further that 'in the present passage it may mean that TM was written less than four years after the attack under Varus.'[35] We have suggested above that *The Gabriel Revelation* was written shortly after 4 BCE. Thus, it seems that TM and *The Gabriel Revelation* were probably written at about the same time.

The main difference between the two texts seems to lie in their attitude to the leaders of the revolt of 4 BCE. In the surviving chapters of TM, these leaders are not mentioned and Taxo is a non-militant model.[36] In contrast, according to our interpretation, *The Gabriel*

---

[31]   6 CE (*Ant* 18, 4–10).

[32]   TM 7:1, Priest, 'Testament of Moses,' 930.

[33]   Atkinson, 'Taxo,' 461–462. See also Atkinson, 'Herod the Great as Antiochus Rededvivus,' in *Of Scribes and Sages*, ed. C. A. Evans (London: T&T Clark, 2004), 141.

[34]   Charles, Apocrypha, 419.

[35]   J. J. Collins, 'The Date and Provenance of the Testament of Moses' in *Studies on the Testament of Moses*, 17 no. 8. See also Atkinson, 'Taxo,' 461–462.

[36]   See, Collins, 'The Date and Provenance of the Testament of Moses,' 30; Collins, 'The Testament (Assumption) of Moses,' 148–149. It is possible that this non-militant conception is a result of the crushing of the revolt and the killing of its leaders; see D. M. Rhoads, 'The assumption of Moses and Jewish History,' in *Studies on the Testament of Moses*, 56–57.

Revelation expresses great admiration for these leaders, particularly Simon of Transjordan. At the same time, both compositions agree that the final salvation will follow the battle of the heavenly army[37] and will not be brought about by human hands.

---

[37] I accept the view that the *nuntius* in TM 10:2 is an angel, probably Michael. See Collins 'The Testament (Assumption) of Moses,' 156; Atkinson, 'Taxo,' 472–473.

Chapter 3

The 'Antichrist' Figures in
The Gabriel Revelation and Related Texts

1. Who is the Wicked Branch?

The dating of the composition of *The Gabriel Revelation* to the period around the beginning of the Common Era sheds new light on the prophecy about the breaking of evil and the 'wicked branch,' mentioned in lines 20–22 of *The Gabriel Revelation*. As we have seen in the commentary, the prophecy on the breaking of evil is based on Daniel 8:25 'but by no human hand, he shall be broken.' It thus seems that the author of *The Gabriel Revelation* had identified the 'wicked branch' with the 'king of bold countenance' of Daniel 8:23. For a Jew writing after the cruel and bloody crushing of the rebellion in 4 BCE, the wicked 'king of bold countenance' refers to the Roman emperor who sent his army to crush the revolt, i.e. Augustus. But if this is the case, why did the author of *The Gabriel Revelation* describe Augustus as a deceiver who represents himself as a 'branch', i.e. messianic savior, but is actually an evil branch?

Augustus was a self-proclaimed *divi filius* – the son of the deified.[1] His claim to divinity was based both on his being the adopted son of the deified Julius Caesar and on the legend regarding his conception by the dragon Apollo.[2] Augustus was depicted in Roman literature and art as the savior of humanity.[3] After the battle of Actium, an imperial cult of Augustus was established in various parts of the Roman Empire.[4]

The author of *The Gabriel Revelation* rejects theses claims of Augustus. He is not a savior and a 'son of god' but rather an 'evil

---

[1] See below, n. 17.
[2] See below, nn. 28–34.
[3] See K. Galinski, *Augustan Culture* (Princeton: Princeton University Press, 1996), 90 ff.
[4] See below, nn. 40, 42.

branch.' He is a deceiver who poses as a righteous king but is in truth a cruel and merciless tyrant.

A similar perception of Augustus is to be found, in my view, in a text discovered in the caves at Qumran known as the 'son of god' text.[5]

4Q246 or the 'son of god' text

This Qumran document is written in Aramaic,[6] and reads as follows:

4Q246 col. 1

.1 ע[לוהי שרת נפל קדם כרסיא

.2 מ[לכא]ל[עלמא אתה רגז ושניך

.3]רא חזוך וכלא אתה עד עלמא

.4 ר[ברבין עקה תתא על ארעא

.5]ונחשירין רב במדינתא

.6]מלך אתור [ומ]צרין

.7]רב להווא על ארעא

.8 י [עבדון וכלא ישמשון

.9 ר[בא יתקרא ובשמה יתכנה

---

[5] The document is known as 4Q246, officially published in E. Puech, '4Q apocryphe de Daniel ar,' *DJD XVII*, Oxford (1996): 165–184. See also the bibliographical lists in *ibid.*, note 1 and F. Garcia Martinez, 'The Messianic Figures in the Qumran Texts,' in *Current Research and Technological Developments in the Study of the Dead Sea Scrolls*, eds. D. W. Parry and S. R. Ricks (Leiden: Brill, 1996), 25, note 16. In the same collection of articles, see also F. M. Cross, 'Notes on the Doctrine of the Two Messiahs at Qumran and the Extracanonical Daniel Apocalypse' (4Q246), 1–13. One should also note some other articles which have appeared recently: E. M. Cook, '4Q246,' *BBR* 5 (1995): 43–66; and J. J. Collins, 'The Background of the 'Son of God' Text,' *BBR* 7 (1997): 51–61; E. Puech, 'Some Remarks on 4Q246 and 4Q521 and Qumran Messianism,' in *The Provo Conference on the Dead Sea Scrolls*, eds. D. W. Parry and E. Ulrich (Leiden: Brill, 1999), 545–565; A. Shteudel, 'The Eternal Reign of the People of God,' *RQ* 17 (1996): 514–516. Both the discussion of this text and the following discussion of the Antichrist figure in the book of Revelation are based on my book *The Messiah before Jesus* (Berkeley: University of California Press, 2000), 32–42, 87–94. I believe that the assumption I made there regarding the identification of the Antichrist figure with Augustus is supported now by the discovery of *The Gabriel Revelation*. I have added several new observations to the current discussion and also tried to respond to some of the objections raised by reviewers of that book.

[6] Unless otherwise stated, the translation of the texts and the reconstruction are taken from Puech's article (above, n. 5), 547.

col. 2

1. ברה די אל יתאמר ובר עליון יקרונה בזיקיא
2. די חזותא כן מלכותהן תהוה שנין[ן] ימלכון על
3. ארעא וכלא ידשון עם לעם ידוש ומדינה למדינ[נ]ה
4. Vacat עד יקום עם אל וכלא יניח מן חרב vacat
5. מלכותא מלכות עלם וכל ארחתיה בקשוט ידי[ן]
6. ארעא בקשט וכלא יעבד שלם חרב מן ארעא יסף
7. וכל מדינתא לה יסגדון אל רבא באילה
8. הוא ועבד לה קרב עממין ינתן בידה וכלהן
9. ירמה קדמוהי שלטנה שלטן עלם וכל תהומי

The English translation is as follows:[7]

col. 1.

1. [   ] on him settled; He fell before the throne,
2. [and said to him, 'Live O k]ing forever! You are disturbed and your [appearance] changed
3. [And I shall interpret O kin]g your dream and all that comes to pass unto perpetuity.
4. ... Through] strong [kings] oppression shall come on the earth.
5. [It will be war between people] and great slaughters in the provinces.
6. [The kings will arise] and the king of Assur and of Egypt [will unite.]
7. [Another/last king will arise and himself] he will be great on the earth.
8. [The kings] will do[peace with him] and all will serve [him.
9. [The son of the gr]eat [Lord][8] he will be called and by this name he will be surnamed.

col. ii

1. The son of God he will be called and the son of the Most High they will call him. Like comets

---

7   The translation is based on the studies of Puech and Cross (above, n. 5).
8   Cross suggests restoring 'king' here, but I have followed E. Puech, *DJD* XXII Oxford (1996): 169.

2. that you saw, so will be their kingdom. For years they will rule on
3. the earth and they will trample all: people will trample on people and province on province.
4. [vacat] Until the people of God arise and make everyone rest from the sword [vacat]
5. Its kingdom is an everlasting kingdom and all its ways are in truth. It will judge
6. the earth with truth, and all will make peace. The sword will cease from the earth,
7. And all the provinces will pay it homage. The great God himself will be its strength and He will make war on its behalf.
8. He will give nations in its hands and all of them
9. He will cast down before it. Its sovereignty is an everlasting sovereignty and all ...

We will now try to clarify the meaning of this text:

The document begins with a seer's appeal to a king.[9] The seer describes future wars:

4Q246 col. 1

4. [... Through] strong [kings] oppression will come on the earth.
5. [it will be war between people] and great slaughters in the provinces.

In connection with this period of wars, a king of Syria and of Egypt is mentioned. After the time of wars, a new king would arise, and all peoples would make peace with him and serve him. This king would be called 'the son of God and son of the Most High':

7. [Another/last king will arise and himself] he will be great over the earth

---

9   This element follows, of course, the pattern of the book of Daniel.

8. [The kings] will do [peace with him] and all will serve [him.
9. [The son of the gre]at [Lord] he will be called and by this name
   he shall be surnamed.[10]

4Q246 col. 2

1. 'The son of God he will be called and the son of the Most High
   they will call him .... '

Shifting to the plural, the document describes kings whose reign
would 'be like comets.' These kings would rule the earth for years
and trample it underfoot.[11]

The following paragraph describes the rise of the people of God,
who would usher in an era of true peace and righteous judgment.
They would be granted everlasting dominion and all states would bow
down to them:

4. [vacat] Until the people of God arise and will make everyone rest
   from the sword. [vacat]
5. Its kingdom is an everlasting kingdom, and all its ways in truth. It
   will jud[ge]
6. the earth with truth, and all will make peace. The sword will cease
   from the earth,
7. and all the provinces will pay it homage. The great God himself will
   be its strength and He will make war on his behalf.
8. He will give nations in its hands and all of them
9. He will cast down before it. Its sovereignty is an everlasting
   sovereignty and all ...

The intriguing question posed by this text is this: who is this figure
called the 'son of God' whom all peoples would make peace with and
serve, and what is his relationship to Jesus?[12]

---

10 Here I have followed Cross's translation (above, n. 5). Puech translates: 'and by this
    name he will be designated.'
11 Col. 2 Cross: (1). '... Like comets (2) that you saw.' Puech translates: 'like the meteors of
    the vision), so will be their kingdom. For years they will rule on (3) the earth and they
    will trample all: People will trample on people and province on province.'
12 Because of the structural similarity between this document and Daniel 7, Milik reached
    the conclusion that the 'son of God' was the wicked king who would be succeeded by

The solution to the mysterious identity of the 'son of God' lies, I believe, in an understanding of the historical background of the period in which this text was written. It is customary to date the time of writing of the Qumran documents based on paleographical testing – that is, according to the form of its script. Such tests show that our document was written around 25 BCE.[13] But the time of the document's inscription is not necessarily identical to the time that the work it contains was composed. The inscription could be the copy of a work written earlier.[14]

the 'people of God'. See J. T. Milik, 'Les modeles arameens du livre d'Esther dans la Grotte 4 de Qumran,' *RQ* 15 (1992): 383–384. E. Puech, who put out the document as part of the official publication of the Qumran literature, has recently declared himself in agreement with this view. Milik and Puech thought that the figure described here was a historical figure. Milik suggested that it was the Seleucid monarch Alexander Balas (150–145 BCE), who called himself the 'son of God.' I find this suggestion untenable: the 'Son of God' is described in this text as a king who will be great on earth, with which all kings will make peace and whom they will serve. This description does not fit the historical figure of Alexander Balas who was not a great king over the earth and was not served by all. Puech and Steudel (above, n. 2) have suggested that the 'Son of God' might have been Antiochus IV. However, this king was not called 'the Son of God.' Other scholars disagree with the view that considers this figure to be negative. Is it possible, they ask, that exalted titles like 'son of God and son of the Most High' can apply to a wicked king, and, if so, how is it that these titles are used in the Gospel of Luke to describe the figure of Jesus? These scholars consequently conclude that the 'son of God' in the Qumran document must be a positive messianic figure. See the articles by Cross and Collins mentioned in note 2. The problem with this view was correctly pointed out by Puech and Steudel: an understanding of the Son of God as a positive messianic figure is connected with the division of the text into four units I 4–6, I 7–II 1a, II Ib–3, II4–9. However, the text is divided by the vacat into two units only and there is no evidence of an additional division in II1. J. J. Collins claims that the notion that the vacat in column two marks a single turning point in the text is 'simplistic.' He brings the example of Daniel 12, where the rise of Michael is followed by a time of distress. In the same way here, he argues, the appearance of the positive 'son of God' is followed by distress caused by wicked kings (See, J. J. Collins, 'An Essene Messiah?' in *Christian Beginnings and the Dead Sea Scrolls*, eds. J. J. Collins and C. A. Evans (Grand Rapids, Michigan: Baker Academic, 2006), 43.) I think, however, that the situation is different in the two cases: In Daniel 12:1 we find a short statement about the 'rise' of Michael, which is followed by the reference to both the distress and the delivery of those who are 'written in the book.' Therefore, one can argue that the rise of Michael is connected especially to this delivery. In the Qumranic document, however, we do not hear a word about salvation before the vacat. The syntax of the first line of column 2 does not support the suggestion that we have here a transition between the positive period of the the 'son of God' and the negative period of some evil kings. I fully agree with Collins' notion in relation to the 'son of God' (*ibid.*, 44) that 'the closet parallel to the terminology is in the Gospel of Luke.' However, this does not prove that the 'Son of God' here is a positive figure. As I will explain in the last section of this chapter, we find here evidence for the impact of the Augustan image on early Christianity, a fact already noted by several scholars.

[13] Puech, 166.

[14] This was the opinion of Milik, for instance, who identified the 'son of God' with one of the Seleucid monarchs.

I believe that the apocalyptic work in this document was written in the Roman period and opine that the content of the work can be clearly understood in light of the political climate in the Roman Empire of the second half of the first century BCE.

Let us review the events of this period: In the year 44 BCE, Julius Caesar was assassinated. In his will, Caesar had adopted Octavian, the son of his niece, as his own son. The adopted son was now given the name of the assassinated emperor: CAESAR OCTAVIANUS. In order to glorify Caesar's memory, Octavian organized games in his honor in July of 44 BCE. During the games, a comet appeared in the sky for seven consecutive nights, causing a great stir among the Roman populace. The comet, called *Caesaris astrum* or *sidus Iulium*, was regarded by the Romans as the soul of Caesar that had ascended to heaven and become a god. The episode was described in Octavian's memoirs:

> During the very time of my games, a comet was seen for seven days in the northern region of the sky. It would rise about the eleventh hour and was very bright ... This comet, the people thought, indicated that Caesar's soul had been received among the immortal gods. For this reason, this symbol was placed above the head of the statue of Caesar which I consecrated in the Forum soon afterwards.[15]

The comet was not only regarded as a sign of Julius Caesar's divine status, but as the sign of the dawning of a new era, a 'golden age,'[16] and as an indication of the divine nature of the new ruler, Octavian.[17] Octavian, who wished to stress that he was the son of the 'divine Julius,' proclaimed himself '*divi filius.*' The title, meaning 'son of God' or 'son of the deified,' appeared on his coins.[18]

---

[15]   Pliny, N. H. II, 94. See Suet. Iul. 88; Dio, 45.7.1; Servius on Vergil, Eclogues, 9. 46.

[16]   On the 'golden age' and Augustus, see K. Galinski, *Augustan Culture* (Princeton: Princeton University Press, 1996), 91 ff.

[17]   On the comet and its significance, see L. R. Taylor, *The Divinity of the Roman Emperor* (Middletown: The American Philological Association, 1931), 90–92, 112–114; S. Weinstock, *Divus Julius* (Oxford: Clarendon Press, 1971), 370–384; D. Fishwick, *The Imperial Cult in the Latin West* (Leiden: Brill, 1987), 74; and P. Zanker, *The Power of Images in the Age of Augustus* (Ann Arbor: University of Michigan Press, 1988), 34–35.

[18]   See Taylor, 106 and Fishwick, 76. Octavian begun to use this title around the year 40 BCE.

The years after Caesar's murder were followed by cruel wars. At first, Octavian and Mark Anthony fought together against Caesar's killers and their supporters. Once they had overcome these enemies, they divided the Empire between them. Octavian was based in Rome and ruled over the Western Empire, while Mark Anthony was based in Alexandria and ruled over Egypt, Syria and the eastern provinces. Mark Anthony's close relations with Cleopatra, Queen of Egypt, caused much friction between the two rulers, and their rivalry ultimately led to the sea battle at Actium in 31 BCE. After Anthony and Cleopatra were defeated by Octavian's fleet, they fled to Alexandria and committed suicide there.

Octavian was now the sole ruler of the Empire. He received the title 'Augustus' – the 'exalted one' – and in many of the Empire's provinces temples and altars were erected, where he was worshipped as a god. In the wake of the battle of Actium the Empire enjoyed peaceful times, and a period of tranquility and prosperity began.

I believe that the Qumran document is related to the events of the period, beginning with the murder of Caesar in 44 BCE through to the decade following the battle of Actium. The work's opening describes a time of war and great distress, and it is in this context that the 'king of Syria and Egypt' is mentioned. This troubled time was the period of cruel wars that raged between the years 44–31 BCE, and the 'king of Syria and Egypt' was none other than Mark Anthony who ruled over these countries. The document then describes the rise of the figure called the 'son of God:'

[Another king will arise, and himself] he will be great on the earth.
[The kings] will do [peace with him] and all will serve [him].
[The son of the gre]at [Lord] he will be called, and by his name he shall be surnamed.
The son of God he will be called and son of the Most High they will call him.
Like comets that you saw, so will be their kingdom.

Augustus was the king who was 'great on the earth' and whom all would serve. He was the sole ruler of the Roman Empire, worshipped as a god by his subjects. Augustus was described as 'son of the great Lord' because he was adopted as a son by the great ruler Julius Caesar, given his name and called CAESAR OCTAVIANUS. And finally, the titles 'son of God' and 'son of the Most High' also refer to Augustus who, as we have seen, was called *divi filius* – the son of God. Here the document shifts to the plural form, stating, 'Like comets that you saw, so will be their kingdom.' The plural form refers to the 'great Lord' and his adopted son: that is, Julius Caesar and Augustus. The writer compares the reign of Caesar and Augustus to comets. The comet is the star that appeared at the time of the games given by Augustus in honor of Caesar's memory, and which became a symbol of Caesar's divinity and of the rule of Augustus. The text continues: 'For years they will rule on the earth and they will trample all.' Caesar and Augustus ruled the earth for many years, trampling and oppressing the Empire's residents and imposing heavy taxes on them. The use of the word 'trampled' reflects the opinion of the writer, who identified Rome with the fourth beast in Daniel's vision, which, it was said, would devour and trample the whole earth.[19] But the writer expected that the oppressive rule of Rome would come to an end and be replaced by the everlasting kingdom of the people of God, which was for him the Danielic 'son of man.'

Augustus now commanded the mighty Roman Empire that comprised a large number of provinces. Many people of his generation deemed him a savior and redeemer who brought peace to the world. As we read in Suetonius, Cicero, the famous writer and rhetorician, saw Augustus in a dream being let down from heaven with chains of gold.[20] Jews of the period, who were looking for the fulfillment of Biblical prophecy, might have regarded Augustus as the realization of the prophecy of 'the son of man coming in the clouds of heaven'

---

[19] See Daniel 7:23. This notion of Rome as the fourth beast that tramples the whole earth is in agreement with the description of the Romans in *Pesher Habakkuk* found in Qumran:

> ... who trample the earth with their horses and with their beasts. And from a distance they come, from the islands of the sea, to devour all the peoples like an eagle, and there is no satiety ... they divide up their yoke and their forced service – their food – upon all the peoples year by year to lay waste many lands.' (*Pesher Habakkuk* 3:9–12, 6:6–8)

[20] Suetonius, *The Twelve Caesars*, 'The Divine Augustus,' 94.

who would be given power and kingship, and whom all peoples and tongues would worship as a god (Daniel 7: 13–14).[21] The author of the Qumran document, however, disagreed with this view. Augustus, who presented himself as the redeemer of humanity, was in his opinion no more than a conqueror and oppressor. Augustan peace was not genuine, since it was achieved by oppressing and trampling underfoot the peoples vanquished by the Romans. The reign of Augustus was a transitory occurrence. True peace and redemption would only come with the appearance of the genuine 'son of man,' the people of God:

> Until the people of God *will arise and will make everyone rest from the sword*. Its kingdom is an everlasting kingdom and all its ways are in *truth*. It will judge the earth with *truth*, and *all will make peace. The sword will cease from the earth*.

The above passage places much emphasis on peace and truth. It seems that the author wishes to say that truth and genuine peace are absent from the Augustan Empire and will only emerge after Augustus' dominion will be replaced by that of the 'people of God'.

I am in full agreement with B. McGinn[22] who noted that this text 'could be the missing link between the picture of Antiochus IV found in Daniel, and the Jewish traditions that may be reflected in such early Christian documents as 2 Thessalonians (2:1–12) and the Little Apocalypse of the Synoptic Gospels (see Matt. 24:1–25:46; Mk. 13:1–37; Luke 21:5–38).'

---

[21] See The description of Augustus as the redeemer of humanity in Philo's *De Legatione ad Gaium*, 143–147.

[22] B. McGinn, *Antichrist, Two Thousand Years of the Human Fascination with Evil* (San Francisco: Harper Collins,1994), 30. On the recent scholarly debate with regard to the origins of the Antichrist, see G. C. Jenks, *The Origins and Early Development of the Antichrist Myth* (Berlin: de Gruyter, 1991); G. W. Lorein, *The Antichrist Theme in the Intertestamental Period, Journal for the Study of the Pseudepigrapha Supplement Series* 44 (London/New York: T&T Clark, 2003).

2. The Antichrist in the Book of Revelation

The book of revelation in the NT was probably written around the year 80 CE.[23] However, scholars have concluded that the author had used sources written earlier in that century.[24] In the following section I would like to claim that some of these materials where borrowed from an apocalypse that dates approximately to the same years of *The Gabriel Revelation*'s composition, and that its author shared many of the views expressed in *The Gabriel Revelation*.

In chapter 13 of the Book of Revelation we read the famous vision of the two beasts: The first beast, with seven heads and ten horns, rose out of the sea. One of the heads of this beast was mortally wounded, but the mortal wound was healed. All the inhabitants of the earth worshipped this beast. Later, a second beast arose: 'Then I saw another beast which rose out of the earth; it had two horns like a lamb and it spoke like a dragon' (Revelation 13:11). By means of signs and miracles, including having fire descend from heaven, this beast persuaded all the inhabitants of the earth to worship the first beast. 'It exercises all the authority of the first beast in its presence, and makes the earth and its inhabitants worship the first beast, whose mortal wound was healed. It works great signs, even making fire come down from heaven to earth in the sight of men' (13:12–13).

Throughout the history of Christianity, many interpretations have been suggested for the vision of the two beasts, but it seems that until now no truly convincing explanation has been offered. In my opinion, the key to understanding the vision is to acknowledge that John, the author of the Book of Revelation, who appears to have written the book in the late first century CE, made use here of an older composition written close to the turn of that century, during the reign of Augustus.

---

[23] See the survey of recent scholarship and discussion of the subject in Thomas B. Slater, 'On the Social Setting of the Revelation of John', *New Testament Studies* 44 (1998): 232–256.

[24] The notion that John, the author of the Book of Revelation, used Jewish sources in his book, has been raised many times in scholarly literature: see D. E. Aune, 'Revelation 1–5,' *Word Biblical Commentary* (Dallas: Word Books, 1997), cx–cxvii. From John's point of view, this material was in keeping with his criticism of the imperial cult and his conception of freedom. See E. Schuessler-Fiorenza, *The Book of Revelation, Justice and Judgement* (Philadelphia: Fortress Press, 1985), 35–84.

The second beast is described as having two horns like a lamb's and speaking like a dragon (Revelation 13:11). This strange combination of a dragon and a lamb's horns[25] can be adequately explained by the propaganda relating to Augustus' divine origin. The figure of a boy or a goat with two horns – the Capricorn – played an important role in the myth of Augustus' divinity. The Capricorn was the sign of the month of Augustus' conception. Suetonius ascribes the importance that Augustus attributed to the sign of the Capricorn to what the astrologer Theogenes told him in his youth:

At Apollonia, Augustus and Agrippa together visited the house of Theogenes the astrologer, and climbed upstairs to his observatory; they both wished to consult him about their future careers. Agrippa went first and was prophesied such an almost incredibly good fortune that Augustus expected a far less encouraging response, and felt ashamed to disclose his nativity. Yet when at last, after a deal of hesitation, he grudgingly supplied the information for which both were pressing him, Theogenes rose and flung himself at his feet; and this gave Augustus so implicit a faith in the destiny awaiting him that he even ventured to publish his horoscope, and issued a silver coin struck with the Capricorn, the sign under which he had been born.[26]

The Capricorn does indeed appear on various coins minted by Augustus. On a coin minted in Spain appears a two-horned goat holding a globe, with the inscription 'Augustus' underneath. Augustus also placed the sign of the Capricorn on some of the standards of the Roman legions. As classicist J. R. Fears explained,[27]

[25] It is possible that in the original text they were goat's horns, and that John, the author of the book, changed the goat into a lamb in order to point at the contrast between Jesus, described as a lamb, and the Antichrist, who looks like a lamb but speaks like a dragon. See J. Jeremias, *TDNT*, I, 341.

[26] Suetonius, Augustus, 94. Suetonius was not consistent here as in section 5 he claimed that Augustus was born in September. The Capricorn was the sign of his conception and not of his birth. See G. W. Bowersock, 'The Pontificate of Augustus,' in *Between Republic and Empire*, eds. A. Raaflaub and M. Toher (Berkeley: University of California Press, 1990), 386.

[27] J. R. Fears, *The Divine Election of the Emperor as a Political Concept at Rome* (Rome: The American Academy at Rome, 1977), 207–210. For a detailed discussion of the various implications of Augustus' use of the sign of the Capricorn, see T. S. Barton, *Power Knowledge* (Ann Arbor: University of Michigan Press, 1994), 40–44.

the Capricorn signified that Augustus reigned with the favor of the gods and had been chosen by them to rule the world.

The beast with the two lamb's horns was described as speaking like a dragon. The dragon symbolized Augustus' connection with the god Apollo.[28] The Roman historian Dio Cassius claimed that Julius Caesar chose Augustus as his successor because he was influenced by a story told by Attia, mother of Augustus and Julius Caesar's niece, that she had conceived him from the god Apollo:

> He was influenced largely by Attia's emphatic declaration that the youth had been engendered by Apollo, for while sleeping once in his temple, she said, she thought she had an intercourse with a dragon and it was this that caused her at the end of the allotted time to bear a son. (Dio Cassius, *Roman History* 45.1.2)

Suetonius, who also related this story in his *History of the Twelve Caesars* (Augustus, 94), added that after the incident in the temple, a dragon-shaped spot appeared on Attia's body. The dragon symbolized Apollo's title, the 'Pythic Apollo,' which he gained when he slew the Python, the terrible dragon that dwelled at Delphi.[29]

The legend of the miraculous birth of Augustus first appeared in an epigram written by Domitius Marsus, a poet who was one of the ruler's friends.[30] Augustus became even more closely connected with the god after his victory at Actium, which took place near the temple of Apollo. The contemporary poet Propertius described the god Apollo as standing on Octavian's vessel and shooting arrows at Cleopatra's ships.[31] After this victory, Augustus constructed an impressive temple to Apollo on the Palatine Hill near his residence.[32] On one of the colonnades near this temple, a statue of Apollo was erected bearing the likeness of Augustus,[33] and in coins minted in Asia Minor after the battle of Actium Augustus was represented as Apollo.[34]

---

[28] J. Gage, *Apollon romain* (Paris: Les Belles Lettres, 1955), 583–637; E. Simon, *Die Portlandvase* (Mainz: Römisch-Germanisches Museum, 1957), 30 ff.

[29] On Apollo's struggle with the Python, see J. Fontenrose, *Python: a Study of Delphic Myth and Its Origins* (Berkeley: University of California Press, 1959).

[30] See S. Weinstock, *Divus Julius* (Oxford: Clarendon Press, 1971),14.

[31] Propertius IV, 6, 27 ff.

[32] On the temple of Apollo and Augustus, see K. Galinski, *Augustan Culture*, 213–224.

[33] Taylor, *The Divinity of the Roman Emperor*, 154 and n. 27.

[34] Fishwick, *The Imperial Cult in the Latin West*, 81, n. 70.

The beast with the two lamb's horns that spoke like a dragon was Augustus, who presented himself as Apollo. The god Apollo was known for his gifts of prophecy, expressed most notably by the oracle at Delphi. Powers of prophecy were likewise ascribed to Augustus.[35] The author of the vision in the Book of Revelation was arguing against Augustus' propaganda, maintaining that Augustus was not a genuine prophet but a false one who spoke like a dragon. The prophesying dragon was the Python,[36] the monstrous serpent that dwelt in the cave at Delphi and was slain by the god Apollo. While Augustus used the myth of Apollo to impart the god's divinity to himself, the author of the vision used the same myth in order to represent Augustus as a monstrous dragon![37]

In the vision of the two beasts, the false prophet persuaded all the inhabitants of the earth to worship the image of the first beast (Revelation 13:12). As R. H. Charles explained at length,[38] the first beast was the Roman Empire. The writer said that one of its heads was mortally wounded, but the beast had recovered from the blow. The mortal blow was that of the conspirators who assassinated Julius

[35] Suetonius, 96–97.

[36] On the prophetic powers ascribed to the Python, see Fontenrose, *Python: a Study of Delphic Myth and Its Origins*, 374. Fontenrose, 375 ff., speaks of the close connection between the Python and Dionysius. As we know, Mark Anthony saw himself as Dionysius: perhaps the author of the vision wished here to turn the myth of Augustus on its head. Augustus compared himself to Apollo, who defeated the Python-Dionysius, but in fact, says the author, he himself was a dragon like the Python-Dionysius!

[37] In A. Yarbro Collins, *The Combat Myth in the Book of Revelation*, Harvard Dissertations in Religion (Missoula: Scholars Press, 1976), 64 ff, Yarbo Collins noticed that the episode in Chapter 12 of the Book of Revelation, discussing the dragon that persecuted the woman who bore the Messiah, was based on the myth of the Python, which persecuted Leto, the mother of Apollo. In her opinion (128), the author of the vision was a Jew who wrote this work in Asia Minor in the first century CE. This story, she claimed (188–189), reflected a polemic against the propaganda disseminated by Augustus and the Caesars who followed him. The author asserts that the Roman Caesar is not Apollo, as he boastfully claims, but the dragon Python. The true Apollo is the Jewish Messiah. Yarbro Collins' suggestions are convincing. It would seem that the story of the persecution of the mother of the Messiah by the dragon and the vision of the two beasts in Chapter 13 originated with the same writer. This writer was familiar with the mythology concerning the god Apollo and with the stories connected with the temple at Delphi. He exploited this knowledge in order to assail Augustus' propaganda. John, the author of the Book of Revelation, included the vision of the two beasts in chapter 13 of his book, making various additions to the original vision. Among these, one must include the reference to Jesus in verse 8 and the hints of the forced imposition of the Caesar cult in verses 9 and 15. If the 'number of the beast' in verse 18 refers to this cult, this verse is also one of John's additions.

[38] R. H. Charles, 'The Revelation of St. John,' *ICC* (1994): 345–346; W. J. Harington, 'Revelation,' *SACRA PAGINA* 16 (1993): 140.

Caesar.[39] But the Roman Empire recovered from this setback and continued to dominate the world. Hence, the image of the first beast, the same image that the false prophet persuaded all the inhabitants of the earth to worship, was the statue of the Roman Empire. This is explained by Suetonius,[40] who reported that in the temples erected in his honor Augustus commanded that a statue of the goddess *Roma* (Rome), the symbol of the Roman Empire, be placed next to that of the Emperor. Augustus was the false prophet of the imperial cult of the statue of *Roma*!

In the vision of the two beasts in Revelation 13, one finds a polemic against the Augustan propaganda,[41] which represents Augustus as a ruler with divine attributes, and against the imperial cult that existed in his time.[42]

3. The Slaying of the Witnesses: Messiahs and their Subsequent Resurrection

In chapter 11 of the Book of Revelation we find the story of the death and resurrection of the two 'witnesses:' 'And I will grant my two witnesses power to prophesy for one thousand two hundred and sixty days, clothed in sackcloth.'

The sackcloth attire is a sign of mourning and sorrow, often combined with adorning ashes.[43] Thus, that the witnesses are dressed in sackcloth may be compared to the 'ashes and sign of exile' in *The Gabriel Revelation,* line 37. In both cases we have a symbol of the hardship and sorrow that precedes the coming of salvation. This is reflected in the number of the days in which the witnesses were dressed in sackcloth: one thousand two hundred and sixty days are

---

[39] See the references in Charles, *ibid.*, 349. Charles disagrees with this interpretation, arguing that, according to verse 3, the mortal wound only affected one of the heads and not the entire beast. This claim though is not decisive. Verses 12 and 14 specifically state that the wound endangered the beast's very existence.

[40] Suetonius, *Augustus*, 52. See also G. W. Bowersock, *Augustus and the Greek World* (Oxford: Clarendon Press, 1965), 116.

[41] Writings of this kind apparently also existed among Greeks who opposed Augustus' rule. See Bowersock, *ibid.*, 110.

[42] On the imperial cult in Asia Minor, see S. F. R. Price, *Rituals and Power, The Roman Imperial Cult in Asia Minor* (Cambridge: Cambridge University Press, 1984)

[43] See Isaiah 58:5; Jeremiah 6:26; Jonah 3:6; Esther 4:1, 3; Daniel 9:3.

three and a half years. This is a clear reference to the time of the subjection of Israel in the book of Daniel (7:25, 12:7).

The Book of Revelation adds more color to the picture of the witnesses: 'These are the two olive trees and the two lamp stands which stand before the Lord of the earth' (11:4). Here there is a definite use of the terminology of Zechariah 4:11–14:

> Then I said to him, 'What are these two olive-trees ... ?' ... Then he said, 'These are the two anointed who stand by the Lord of the whole earth.'

The images 'two olive-trees' and 'two anointed' indicate at the Messiah's anointment with anointing oil. The prophet Zechariah hinted here at the two leaders of his period, the return to Zion: The royal Messiah Zerubbabel, son of Shealtiel, and the priestly Messiah, Jeshua the son of Jozadak. This being the case, scholars have suggested that the two witnesses in the Book of Revelation are a royal Messiah and a priestly Messiah.[44] However, in light of the mention of David and Ephraim in *The Gabriel Revelation,* we must consider Torrey's suggestion that the witnesses are the Messiah son of David and the Messiah son of Joseph.[45]

We then find a description of the miracles performed by these two witnesses:

> And if any one would harm them, fire pours out from their mouth and consumes their foes; if any one would harm them, thus he is doomed to be killed.

> They have power to shut the sky, that no rain may fall during the days of their prophesying, and they have power over the waters to turn them into blood, and to smite the earth with every plague, as often as they desire.

The fire that pours out from their mouth is a sign reminiscent of the Davidic Messiah of Isaiah 11:4. The shutting of the sky is similar to

---

[44] See W. H. Brownlee, 'John the Baptist in the New Light of Ancient Scrolls,' in *The New Scrolls and the New Testament,* ed. K. Stendahl (New York: Harper & Row, 1957), 47.

[45] Charles Torrey,'The Messiah Son of Ephraim,' *JBL* 66 (1947): 274–277.

the act of Elijah, while the turning of water into blood reminds us of Moses. We may thus conclude that we have here a combination of Messiahs who are also true prophets. This image sharply contrasts with that of the second beast – a wicked king who is also a false prophet.

Revelation tells further about the killing of these two figures:

'And when they have finished their testimony, the beast that ascends from the bottomless pit will make war upon them and conquer them and kill them' (11:7).

According to the Book of Revelation, the two witnesses/Messiahs were killed[46] by a beast that ascends from an abyss (*abyssos*) (Revelation 11:7), which is probably also a designation for the Roman army.[47]

When did this event take place?

At the beginning of chapter 11 of the Book of Revelation, before the story of the two witnesses, we read:

Then I was given a measuring rod like a staff, and I was told: 'Rise and measure the temple of God and the altar and those who worship there, but do not measure the court outside the temple;

---

46 In the Greek original, the term used for witnesses is martyrs. On the history of the term 'martyr,' see G. W. Bowersock, *Martyrdom and Rome* (Cambridge: Cambridge University Press, 1995), 5–21.

47 The word *abyssos* has various meanings. (On these different meanings, see J. Massyngberde-Ford, *Revelation* (Garden City: Anchor Bible, 1975),152.) *Abyssos* can refer to the depths of the sea, but also the depths of the earth. If we interpret it as referring here to the depths of the earth, we would have to identify the beast ascending from these depths as the second beast in chapter 13, which is described as coming up from the earth (see Flusser, 449, n. 192). That is to say, it is the beast that is also described as a false prophet and so resembles Augustus. But if we interpret the word as referring to the depths of the sea, we would have to identify the beast ascending from the abyss with the first beast of chapter 13, the beast ascending from the sea. See Yarbro Collins, *The Combat Myth in the Book of Revelation*, 165. Of this beast it is said: 'it was allowed to make war on the saints and to conquer them' (13:7). This recalls the statement in chapter 11 about the beast that ascends from the abyss: 'The beast that ascends from the abyss will make war upon them and conquer them and kill them.' We have already identified the beast coming up from the sea as the Roman Empire, which had recovered from the murder of Julius Caesar. Hence, both these possibilities lead to the same conclusion: the two witnesses were killed by the Roman imperial army, the army of Augustus.

leave that out, for it is given over to the nations, and they will trample over the holy city for forty-two months.

We learn here that in the battle in which the two witnesses were killed the Roman soldiers penetrated the courtyard of the Temple, but the Temple itself and the altar remained untouched. This provides us with the key to the event's precise time of occurrence.

As we recall, King Herod died in 4 BCE. After Herod's death on Passover of that year, a great revolt broke out in the country.[48] The revolt was directed against Herod's successor, Archelaus, and the Roman garrison that secured his rule. During the revolt, Roman soldiers entered the courtyard of the Temple and plundered its treasury. The soldiers set fire to the chambers in the courtyard,[49] but did not enter the inner precincts where the altar was situated nor did they penetrate the Temple itself. This account corresponds accurately with the first two verses of Chapter 11 of the Book of Revelation where the courtyard of the Temple has been trampled by the nations, but not the Temple or the altar![50]

---

[48] Josephus, *Jewish Antiquities* 17:213–218; *The Jewish War* 3,1,2.

[49] *Jewish Antiquities* 17: 261–262; *The Jewish War*, 2,3,3. This is the background to Hystaspes' assertion (Lactantius XVII:6) that the wicked king – the 'false prophet' – would try to destroy the Temple.

[50] J. Wellhausen, in *Analyse der Offenbarung Johannis* (Berlin: Weidmann, 1907), thought that these verses expressed the views of the Zealots in the great rebellion against Rome. But in the great rebellion the outer court, the altar and the Temple were all captured (Josephus, *The Jewish War*, 1–6, 4, 6), so that the description in the Book of Revelation does not correspond to the historical reality of 70 CE. On the other hand, the events of 4 BCE perfectly accord with the Book of Revelation. As Charles and other scholars have argued, John, the author of the Book of Revelation, drew on an early Jewish source. As I have pointed out (above, n. 39), the vision of the persecution of the Messiah's mother in chapter 12, the vision of the two beasts in chapter 13 and verses 1–13 of chapter 11 also derive from this source. It is possible that the paragraphs were written by a man whose native language was Hebrew or Aramaic, an idea supported by the large number of Semitic linguistic forms appearing in these sections of the Book of Revelation. See S. Thompson, *The Apocalypse and Semitic Syntax* (Cambridge: Cambridge University Press, 1985), 107 (on chapters 11 and 12). Because the events of the revolt of 4 BCE are reflected here, one can claim with certainty that the work was written after that date; the time of writing seems to be the beginning of the first century CE. As I have noted (n. 37), Yarbro Collins maintains that the Jewish author of the vision of the persecution of the Messiah's mother was based in Asia Minor. I tend to agree with this view. Perhaps the author was a Jew who fled from the land of Israel when the revolt was extinguished and settled in Asia Minor. There he became acquainted with the various legends connected with Apollo prevalent in that area (see Yarbro Collins, 245–252) and made use of them in his criticism of Augustus. A similar case of a Jew who fled from the land of Israel at the time of the crushing of a revolt against the Romans and who settled in Asia Minor is that of Trypho, known for his debate with Justin Martyr. Trypho left the land of Israel at the time of the crushing of the Bar-Kochba rebellion, and settled in Ephesus.

The revolt of 4 BCE was brutally crushed by Quintilius Varus,[51] Augustus' governor in Syria.[52] Varus arrived from Syria with two legions and some other forces. The soldiers of his army wreaked havoc in their wake and abused women;[53] Varus crucified two thousand of the rebels and others were taken prisoner and sold to slavery.[54] The Jews considered Augustus Caesar to be responsible for the brutal suppression of the revolt and the burning of the Temple's courtyard. This is evident in the Testament of Moses (6:9) that attributes all these acts to 'a powerful king of the west.' This figure is not Varus, since Varus was not 'a powerful king' and he approached Jerusalem from Syria, i.e. from the north and not from the east.[55] The 'powerful king of the west' is clearly Augustus, whose army crushed the revolt so mercilessly.

As we have seen in the previous chapter (p. 50), TM speaks about the 'four hours,' an expression that is probably based on Daniel 7:25, 12:7. J. J. Collins suggested on this basis that TM was composed within four years of the revolt of 4 BCE. In Revelation 11:2 we read: 'and they will trample over the holy city for forty-two months'; this is again clearly based on the same scriptures in Daniel. Applying Collins' view also here, we may assume that the Jewish apocalypse used by the author of Revelation was written within four years of the revolt of 4 BCE. For the author of this Jewish Apocalypse, the trampling by the gentiles did not stop with the vanquishing of the revolt; Jerusalem and the Temple were under the 'trample' of the Romans also during the time of Archelaus. Thus, the time measure 'forty-two months' is clearly a prophecy, while the reference to the 'trample' of the gentile on the Temple court is based on the historical event of 4 BCE.

The Book of Revelation continues with the account of the resurrection of the two witnesses:

---

[51] In rabbinical chronography, the revolt was named after him. See Ch. J. Milikowski, *Seder Olam, a Rabbinic Chronography* (PhD dissertation, Yale University, 1981), 441.

[52] On Quintilius Varus, see R. Syme, *Augustan Aristocracy* (Oxford: Clarendon Press, 1986), 313 ff.

[53] See Josephus, *Jewish Antiquities* 17:291–292; *Against Apion*, 1,7.

[54] *Jewish Antiquities* 17: 289, 295; *The Jewish War*, 2,5, *The Testament of Moses* 6:89.

[55] See, G. Hölscher, 'Über die Entstehungszeit der 'Himmelfahrt Moses,' *ZN*, 17 (1916): 111–112.

But after the three and a half days a breath of life from God entered them, and they stood up on their feet, and great fear fell on those who saw them. Then they heard a loud voice from heaven saying to them, 'Come up hither!' And in the sight of their foes they went up to heaven in a cloud. (Revelation 11: 11–12).

The description of the death and resurrection of the witnesses has several points of similarity with the resurrection of the 'prince of the princes' in *The Gabriel Revelation.* The bodies of the two witnesses were not given for burial (11:9). A similar situation is probably reflected in the description of the 'prince of princes' as 'dung.' The different timeframes of 'by three days' in *The Gabriel Revelation* and 'after the three and a half days' in Revelation can be explained by the different biblical contexts: Revelation is again based on Daniel 7:25, 12:7, while *The Gabriel Revelation* relies on Hosea 6:2. The scene in *The Gabriel Revelation* is still associated with the details of an historical event: the mention of the 'rocky crevices' close to that of the death of the 'prince of princes' probably alludes to the killing, in the rocky crevices of Transjordan, of Simon, the messianic leader of the revolt. In contrast, the scene in Revelation seems to be fashioned with more legendary and symbolic elements: the location is changed to Jerusalem (11:8) and it is told that at the time of their ascension an earthquake destroyed a tenth of the city (11:13).

4. Abaddon

The story of the two beasts is told in chapter 13 of the Book of Revelation. Chapter 9 of this book contains another vision that, in my view, is closely related to the 'second beast':

And the fifth angel blew his trumpet, and I saw a star fallen from heaven to earth, and he was given the key of the shaft of the bottomless pit; he opened the shaft of the bottomless pit, and from the shaft rose smoke like the smoke of a great furnace, and the sun and the air were darkened with the smoke from the shaft. Then from the smoke came locusts on the earth, and they were given

power like the power of scorpions of the earth ... In appearance
the locusts were like horses arrayed for battle; on their heads were
what looked like crowns of gold; their faces were like human faces,
their hair like women's hair, and their teeth like lions' teeth; they
had scales like iron breastplates, and the noise of their wings was
like the noise of many chariots with horses rushing into battle. They
have tails like scorpions, and stings, and their power of hurting men
for five months lies in their tails. They have as king over them the
angel of the bottomless pit; his name in Hebrew is Abaddon, and
in Greek he is called Apollyon. (Revelation 9:1–3, 7–11)

It has already been noted[56] that the description of Abaddon, the
'angel of the bottomless pit,' is paralleled in the Dead Sea Scrolls.
In 4Q286 line 7, as part of the yearly curses on Belial, we find the
expression:

מל א[ך] השחת ורו[ח האב[דון

Ange]l of the Pit, and spir[it of Aba]ddon[57]

It is Belial who in the Qumranic document is designated as the
angel of the pit and the spirit of Abaddon. The expressions in Rev.
9:11 'The angel of the pit... Abaddon' are clearly derived from the
Hebrew lexicon. Hence, we may conclude that John, the author of
the Book of Revelation, has here used the same Jewish source that
underlies the passages in 11:1–13; 13:1–14.

Abaddon, the angel of the pit, is here termed Apollyon, meaning
'the destroyer' or 'the exterminator.' Apollyon thus parallels Abaddon,
which means destruction. Apollyon is usually understood as a variation
on Apollo.[58] Apollo–Apollyon is described here as the angel of
the bottomless pit from which smoke arose. In my opinion, this
description is connected to the belief that prevailed in ancient times in
the existence of a deep chasm under the temple of Apollo in Delphi.

---

[56] See P. J. Kobelski, *Melchizedek and Melchiresa*, CBQ Monograph Series 10 (Washington: Catholic Biblical Association of America, 1981), 47.

[57] Kobelski, *ibid.*, 43–44.

[58] See A. Oepke, *TDNT* 1 (1964): 397.

It was also believed that mist emerged from this chasm.[59] Thus, Apollo was described as the god who resides in the deep pit.[60] The description in Revelation 9:1–2 seems to be the destruction of Apollo's temple in Delphi. The description of Apollo as Satan accords with the belief that this god was responsible for pestilence, plagues and disasters.[61]

Apollo's satanic nature is emphasized with regard to Augustus in an anecdote relayed by Suetonius.[62]

> There was besides a private dinner of his, commonly called that of the 'twelve gods,' which was the subject of a gossip. At this, the guests appeared in the guise of gods and goddesses, while he himself was made up to represent Apollo, as was charged not merely in the letters of Antony, who spitefully gives the names of all the guests, but also in these anonymous lines which every one knows:

>> 'As soon as that table of rascals had secured a choragus and Mallia saw six gods and six goddesses while Caesar was impiously playing the playing the false role of Apollo and fasting amid novel debaucheries of the gods, then all the deities turned their faces from the earth and Jupiter himself fled from his golden throne'.

> The scandal of this banquet was the greater because of dearth and famine in the land at the time, and on the following day there was an outcry that the gods had eaten all the grain and that Caesar was in truth Apollo, but Apollo the Tormentor, a surname under which the god was worshiped in one part of the city.

For our purposes, it is not important whether this story actually took place.[63] Rather the description of Octavian-Augustus as Apollo the

---

[59] See A. P. Oppe, 'The Chasm at Delphi,' *JHS* 24 (1904): 214 ff.

[60] See E. R. Dodds, *The Greeks and the Irrational* (Berkeley: University of California Press, 1951), 396–397, n. 66.

[61] See J. Fontenrose, *Python – A Study of Delphic Myth and its Origins* (Berkeley: University of California Press, 1980), 471.

[62] Augustus, 70.

[63] See H. Heinen's discussions, 'Zur Begrundung des romischen Kaiserkultus,' *Klio* 11 (1911): 129–177; L. R. Taylor, *The Divinity of the Roman Empero* (Middletown: The American Philological Association, 1931),119; H. G. Niemeyer, *Studien zur statuarischen Darstellung der romischen Kaiser* (Monumenta Artis Romanae 7) (Berlin: 1968), 54, nn. 448 ff.; S. Weinstock, *Divus Julius* (Oxford: Clarendon Press, 1971), 15; D. Fishwick, *The Imperial Cult in the Latin West* (Leiden: Brill, 1987), 80–81.

Tormentor, a title inspired by Apollo's cruelty, is significant. Apollo won this title after he removed the skin of the satyr Marsyas who had competed with him in musical activities.[64] Augustus was thus described by his Roman rivals as Apollo the Tormentor. It therefore seems that Apollyon the destroyer is the person who in Rome was called Apollo the Tormentor, i.e. Augustus. As in Rev. 13:11, here too we find a critique and parody of Augustus' claim to divinity, which was based on his connection with Apollo. It is also possible that the mention (9:1) of the star that fell from heaven and opened the bottomless pit parodies the comet of Augustus. As we have seen above, this comet was presented as an indication of the divine nature of Octavian–Augustus. Here it causes the satanic bottomless pit to open!

The description of the Augustan army as locust is clearly based on the verses of Joel 2:1–10. As we recall, Joel further calls this locust 'the northerner' (2:20). We have seen that in *The Gabriel Revelation* (lines 41, 56) the enemy is called 'the northerner.' This is another point of similarity between these two compositions.[65]

5. Armilus of the Book of Zerubbabel

We have seen in the first chapter[66] clear linguistic evidence that *The Gabriel Revelation* was known and used by the *Book of Zerubbabel.*

The *Book of Zerubbabel* has been the most influential of the medieval Hebrew apocalypses. It is ascribed to Zerubbabel who was the leader of the Jewish community at the time of the return from the Babylonian Exile.[67] The book in its present form was written in the seventh century,[68]

---

[64] *Apollodorus mythographus,* I. 24.

[65] The revolt of 4 BCE broke out in April and appears to have been crushed in August. See H. W. Hoehner, *Herod Antipas* (Grand Rapids: Zondervan, 1980), 37. Thus, the revolt lasted for some five months. This may have served the reference to the period of five months in Revelation 9:5.

[66] See p. 8.

[67] See Haggai 1:1 Zechariah 4:6 Ezra 2:2 Nehemiah 7:7.

[68] See, I. Levi, 'L'apocalypse de Zorobabel,' *REJ* 68 (1911): 129–160; 69 (1919): 108–121, 71 (1920): 57–65. Y. Even Shmuel, *Midreshei Geulah,* 2nd edn (Jerusalem and Tel-Aviv: 1954), 62–66. I will henceforth refer to Even Shmuel's work as ES. See further, the studies of M. Himmelfarb, 'Sefer Zerubbabel,' in *Rabbinic Fantasies,* eds. D. Stern and M. J. Mirski (Philadelphia: Jewish Publication Society, 1990), 67–90; B. M. Wheeler, 'Imagining the Sasanian Capture of Jerusalem,' *Orientalia Christiana Periodica* 57

but it has been noted[69] that it is based on much earlier sources. Bousset and Flusser have shown that this book is closely connected to the book of Revelation.[70]

Let us begin our discussion of this work by examining its dating. Israel Levi has dated the book to the seventh century CE, mainly because it mentions the name שירוי Shiroi (Shiroe, Siroes), who was King of Persia from February to September 628 CE. Himmelfarb provides another indication for a seventh-century date. One of the book's innovations is the introduction of the figure of Hephzibah, the mother of the Davidic Messiah. She defeats two kings with the help of her miraculous staff and guards the east gate of the wall of Jerusalem after the slaying of the Messiah son of Joseph. Himmelfarb points out the similarity of Hephzibah's role to that assigned to the Virgin at the time of Heraclius.[71] Thus, in Himmelfarb's words, 'the military role assigned to Hephzibah represents an attempt to offer a Jewish answer to the Virgin.'[72]

In my view, however, both Shiroi and Hephzibah, who are pivotal in dating the work to the seventh century, are not integral to the main story related in the book but were interpolated in the text in the course of its final redaction in the seventh century. Himmelfarb comments on the figure of Hephzibah:

> Nowhere else in Jewish speculation is the mother of the Messiah so important a figure, and even here her role has not been fully

---

(1991): 69–85; P. Speck, 'The Apocalypse of Zerubabel and Christian Icons,' *JSQ* 4 (1977): 183–190; J. Dan, 'Armilus: The Jewish Antichrist and the origins of *SEFFER ZERUBBAVEL*,' in *Toward the Millenium*, eds. P. Schafer and M. R. Cohen, (Leiden: Brill, 1998), 73–104. For a discussion of the Galilean motifs in the book see, E. Reiner, 'From Joshua to Jesus,' *Zion* 61 (1996): 298 ff. There is no critical edition of the book. I have used here the three pieces of textual evidence adduced by ES, the fragments in A. J. Wertheimer ed. *BATEI MIDRASHOT*, Vol. 2 (Jerusalem: Ktav VSefer, 1955), 502–505, and the manuscript copies in the collection of the institute for Jewish manuscripts at the Hebrew University, Jerusalem. Geniza fragments of the book were published by S. Hopkins, *A Miscellany of Library Pieces from the Cambridge Geniza Collection* (Cambridge: Cambridge University Library 1978), 10,15, 64–65, 72.

[69]   See, E. Fleischer, '*Haduta-Hadutahu-Chedweta:* Solving an Old Riddle,' *Tarbiz* 53 (1983): 92–93 (Heb.).

[70]   W. Bousset, *The Antichrist Legend* (London: Hutchinson, 1896), 104–111; D. Flusser, *Judaism and the Origins of Christianity* (Jerusalem: Magnes Press, 1988), 425 ff.

[71]   Himmelfarb, 'Sefer Zerubbabel,' 69.

[72]   *Ibid.*

integrated into the traditional picture... Hephzibah fits only uneasily with the by now traditional picture of two Messiahs; she appears first with the Messiah, son of Ephraim and only later with the Davidic Messiah as her son.[73]

This lack of fit is to be explained, in my view, by the assumption that the original story about the killing of the Messiah son of Joseph by Armilus and his resurrection, and the defeat of Armilus by the Messiah son of David predated the seventh century. In the process of the final editing of the book in the seventh century the figure of Hephzibah was interpolated to the story in order to offer a response to the figure of Mary. This late insertion, however, created the uneasiness noted by Himmelfarb.

Shiroi's place and role in the story is also ambiguous;[74] this ambiguity is reflected in differences between the manuscripts. After inspection of all the available textual evidence, we can ascribe them to two different major traditions: One is represented by the Sasson MS. 756, the N.Y. JTS MS. 2325/18, fragment no. 3 in Wertheimer's book,[75] and the first printed version.[76]

According to this tradition, neither Shiroi nor Armilus killed the Messiah son of Joseph. However, immediately after relating the killing of the Messiah son of Joseph, Shiroi disappears and the main plot concerns Armilus and the Messiah son of David. Shiroi reappears only at the book's end, in the list of the ten kings of the eschatological era.[77] Shiroi's end is not related in this tradition. The role of Armilus presents another difficulty in this version. He is a central figure in the book, described as the final enemy to be killed by the Messiah son of David. However, nowhere in this version do we find any description of Armilus' actions against the Jews or against the Messiahs. Why is he then an enemy?

---

[73] *Ibid.*, 69 and n. 8 on 82.
[74] This was already noted by E. Fleischer, 'Solving the Qiliry Riddle,' *Tarbiz* 54 (1985): 404, n. 59.
[75] Wertheimer, *Batei Midrashot*, 504.
[76] Constantinople 1519.
[77] This list seems to be a late effort of harmonization between the figures of Shiroi and Armilus. It makes Shiroi the ninth king and Armilus the tenth.

It seems that these problems surfaced when the figure of Shiroi was imposed on the original story, which related the killing of the Messiah son of Joseph by Armilus. For this reason Armilus was the final enemy. In the seventh century the figure of Shiroi was interpolated in the book. Shiroi was represented as the killer of the Messiah, and this caused the anomaly of Armilus' role in the book.

The second tradition is represented by MS. Oxford Bodl. Heb. 11,[78] MS. Oxford Bodl. 2287/6, MS. Oxford Bodl. 160/2, MS. London 832/8, MS. Rome Casanatense 174/2 and the version published by Yellinek.[79] In this version, Shiroi plays a marginal role. After relating the story of the reign in Jerusalem of the Messiah son of Joseph, whose name is Nehemiah son of Hushiel, the text continues:

> Then in the fifth year of Nehemiah and the gathering of the holy ones, Shiroi, king of Persia will go up against Nehemiah, son of Hushiel and Israel, and there will be great trouble for Israel. Hephzibah ... will go out with the staff that the Lord God of Israel gave her. The lord will give them a spirit of confusion and men will kill their neighbors and brothers. There the wicked one will die.[80]

Thus, in this version Shiroi launches a war against the Messiah son of Joseph but doesn't manage to kill him. Instead, Shiroi is killed by the magic effect of Hephziba's staff. The slaying of the Messiah is assigned in this version to Armilus, who plays the central role of the enemy of Israel.

This version seems to be the result of a renewed editing that sought to reconcile the contradictions found in the first version. As we have seen above, the insertion of Shiroi as the slayer of the Messiah has led to serious problems in the plot. In the second tradition, an effort was made to restore the original plot in which Armilus is the slayer of the Messiah, thus marginalizing Shiroi in the story. The first version can be dated to approximately 728 CE when Siroi was king of Persia;

---

[78] This is according to the present cataloging system. It was previously no. 2797. Levi used this manuscript.

[79] A. Yellinek, *Beit ha-Midrash*, Vol. 2 (1853–78; repr., Jerusalem: 1967): 54–57.

[80] Himmelfarb's translation (74) based on MS. Ox. Bodl. Heb. 11.

the second version should be dated to a later time, when Shiroi lost the throne.[81]

We may conclude that the two figures of Shiroi and Hephzibah, on which the dating of the book to the seventh century was based, are not an integral part of the story. Thus, although we can view their appearance as evidence that the current versions of the book came into being during this period, we can also infer that the original story about the slaying of the Messiah son of Joseph by Armilus predates the seventh century. This agrees with the fact already mentioned that the killing of the Messiah son of Joseph appears in Talmudic sources dating from no later than the third century.

We know of Jewish apocalyptic literature dating from the second century BCE through to the first century CE.[82] Later, in the Talmudic period, it disappeared. In the above versions of the *Book of Zerubbabel* we encounter a revival of Jewish apocalypse in the seventh century.[83] A similar phenomenon is to be observed in another type of literature: the retelling of the biblical epic. Books that retold the biblical stories were also common from the second century BC to the first century CE[84] but are not known in the Talmudic period. We then notice a revival of this type of writing in the seventh or the eighth century. We find it, for instance, in the work *Pirke De-Rabbi Eliezer*.[85] As we may recall, this book, which was written in the seventh or the eighth century, contains many elements drawn from the Second Temple Period.

---

[81]   It is also possible that the second version represents an effort to update the story with the conditions after 628. In the year 629 Heraclius conquered Jerusalem and defeated the Jewish population in the land of Israel. As a Roman-Byzantine Emperor, Heraclius could be identified with Armilus. Hence, it is possible that the second version was motivated by the wish to represent the Roman-Byzantine Emperor as the last enemy and the killer of the Messiah. The second version is already reflected in the poem 'That Day' (אותו היום), probably written in the summer of the year 637 on the eve of the Arab conquest of Jerusalem. See J. Yahlom, 'On the Validity of Literary Works as Historical Source,' *Cathedra* 11 (1979): 125–133. In this poem, the killing of the Messiah son of Joseph is related to הרמל יום – Armilus.

[82]   The book of Daniel, Enoch, The Testament of Moses, The fourth book of Ezra and others.

[83]   See J. Dan, *Ha-Sippur ha-Ivri bi-Ymei ha-Beinayim* (Jerusalem: Keter, 1974), 35–36. For possible reasons for the renaissance of apocalyptic literature in this period, see Flusser, *Judaism*, 425.

[84]   The Book of Jubilees, Joseph and Aseneth, Life of Adam and Eve and others.

[85]   See I. Knohl, 'Cain: Son of God or Son of Satan,' *Jewish Biblical Interpretation in a Comparative Context*, eds. N. B. Dohrmann and D. Stern (Philadelphia: The University of Pennsylvania Press, 2008), 37–52.

I would like to argue here that Armilus, the Antichrist figure of *The Book of Zerubbabel*, originates in the Second Temple Period. In my view, he was probably borrowed from a Jewish apocalypse written at the same time as *The Gabriel Revelation* and the Jewish apocalypse used by the author of Revelation. As the linguistic connection[86] between *The Gabriel Revelation* and the *Book of Zerubbabel* proves, the author of the *Book of Zerubbabel* had access to materials from this period.

The *Book of Zerubbabel* recounts how an angel took Zerubbabel to a large city and told him:

This city is Nineveh, the city of bloodshed, which is the big Rome. And I have said to him: 'When would be the end of these awful things?' And he took me by my hand and brought me to the house of disgrace.[87]

And he showed me there a marble stone in the shape of a very beautiful virgin. And he said to me: 'What do you see, Zerubbabel?' And I said: 'I see a marble stone in the shape of a very beautiful woman.'

And he told me: 'This stone is the wife of Belial, and when Belial sees her, he will lie with her[88] and she will become pregnant and will bear him Armilus, and she will be the chief idolatry.[89] And he (Armilus) will rule over the whole world and his dominion will be from one end of the earth to the other end of the earth. And he will make signs.[90] He will worship strange gods, and will speak words against the Most High and no one will be able to stand against him.[91] And all nations will go astray after him except for Israel.[92]

---

[86] See above, chapter 1. nn. 41–42.

[87] As noted by ES. 448, the version בית החורף (the winter house) is a corruption of בית החורף (the house of disgrace). In some manuscripts we have בית הלצות (the house of merrymaking).

[88] The words 'he will lie with her' are attested in most versions of the book.

[89] Wertheimer, *BATEI MIDRASHOT*, 504. A similar version is to be found in the Geniza fragment, Oxford Bodl. 2642.

[90] Levi's version (ES, 387), says: ועשר אותיות בידו (and ten signs in his hand).

[91] The last two sentences are from the London MS. 832.8. A similar version is to be found in the Rome Casanatense MS. 174.2. In Levi's version (ES, 387) the words ולצד עליון ידבר and (he) will speak words against the Most High (see Daniel 7:25) were corrupted to ולזכר ידבר.

[92] MS Rome Casanatense, *ibid.*

And he, Armilus, will take his mother from the house of disgrace and all places and all nations will worship this stone and will make sacrifices and libations to it. And no one will be able to look upon her face because of her beauty.[93]

He is Arimolaus[94] son of Satan, and he will become a King in Emmaus, the city of his father, and his fear will fall in all places.[95]

Armilus is Romulus,[96] his name clearly referring to a ruler of the Roman Empire. Armilus is described here as the son of Belial or Satan, as one who performs signs and as a king who misleads all peoples. These attributes liken him to the second beast in Revelation and to the second wicked king in the Oracle of Hystaspes, who was born of an evil spirit, makes signs and leads many people astray.[97] The story of Armilus has two unique elements: (1) his mother was a marble stone in the shape of a very beautiful woman, which stood in the house of disgrace in Rome. Armilus later made his mother an

---

93 Levi's version (ES, 389).

94 For this spelling see I. Knohl, 'On "the Son of God,"Armilus and Messiah Son of Joseph,' *Tarbiz* 68 (1998): 33.

95 This is the version in MS 2325/18 of the Jewish Theological Seminary in NY, 194. The Hebrew is:

הוא ארימולאוס בן השטן וימלוך במדינת אביו ששמה אמאוס ובכל המקומות יפול פחדו

There are different versions for this statement in other MS:

ויעל וימלוך באי מום מדינת השטן אביו – the Rome Casanatense MS. 174.2

ויעלה וימלוך באמוס מדינת השטן אביו – Gaster Collection, London no. 942,9

ויעלה וימלוך באימים מדינת השטן אבי בליעל אכיו וכל אחיו יזוער ממנו – Sasson MS 765.5, 32

ויעלה וימלוך באימים מדינתא ושטן אבי בליעל וכל רואיו יזוער ממנו – Levy MS, ES, 389

ויעלה וימלוך באימוס מדינות השטן אשר נטל אביו וכל רואיו יזוער ממנו – Kushta version ES, 382

והוא יבוא בעיר עמואם מדינת אביו ונותן את כסאו עליה – Marmorstein, 'Les signes du Messie,' *REJ* 52 (1906):183. The spelling עמואם in the last version is common to Christian-Aramaic and Arabic sources (see E. Y. Kutscher, *Hebrew and Aramaic Studies*, (Jerusalem: Magnes Press, 1977), 245 (Heb.)). The Hebrew form אמאוס is preserved in the JTS manuscript. All other forms of the city name in the different versions, i.e. אימוס, אימים, אמום, אי מום seem to be derived from spellings like עימום אימוס.

96 A medieval Christian writer (see Bousset, *The Antichrist Legend*, 53), had already identified Armilus with Romulus. Noldeke noted that ארמלאוס is the Syrian form of Romulus: see T. Noldeke, 'Momsen's Darstellung der romischen Herrschaft und romischen Politik im Orient,' *ZDMG* 39 (1895): 343 n. 1. See further, Y. Yahalom, 'On the Validity of Literary Works as Historical Sources,' *Cathedra* 11 (1979): 129 (Heb.); Speck, 'The Apocalypse of Zerubabel and Christian Icons,' 186, n. 12.

97 Lactantius, VII, 17, 2–5 (McGinn, *Apocalyptic Spirituality*, 61–62).

object of worship for all nations; (2) he became king in Emmaus, the city of his father Satan, and he terrified inhabitants everywhere.

I would like to suggest that the figure of Armilus is based on Augustus Caesar. As is well known,[98] the Imperial cult founded by Augustus focused on the images of Augustus and the goddess Roma, who was represented as a beautiful woman. Hence, the marble stone in the shape of a very beautiful woman, which stood in the 'house of disgrace' in Rome can be identified with the goddess Roma. Augustus did indeed turn the goddess Roma into a cult object for many peoples.

Armilus is said to have become king in Emmaus, the city of his father Satan; he is subsequently universally feared. Emmaus is a small town on the way from Jerusalem to the Mediterranean. Why is this town described as the city of Satan? The solution to this riddle is, in my opinion, connected to the various names this place was given. In the third century CE the name Emmaus was changed to Nicopolis,[99] yet both Jews and Christians also continued to use its old name, Emmaus.[100]

We may assume, therefore, that in the original story about Armilus, composed around the turn of the Common Era, he became king in Nicopolis. This referred not to Nicopolis-Emmaus in Judea, but rather to Nicopolis in Greece, which was founded by Augustus to celebrate his great victory at Actium in the year 31 BCE. Nicopolis was founded near Actium and it was there, in Actium-Nicopolis, that Augustus became the sole ruler of the Roman Empire. It was at this moment that he became feared in all places.

In a later period, when the *Book of Zerubabbel* assumed its present form, the original significance of the name Nicopolis was not known. The editor of the book thought it was a reference to Nicopolis in Judea, and hence changed it to the name used by the Jews – Emmaus. The city is described in the *Book of Zerubbabel* as the city of Satan, the father of Armilus. Why is Nicopolis thus described?

[98] See Suetonius, 'Augustus' 52, in *The Lives of the Caesars*, trans. J. C. Rolfe (London: William Heneman, 1913). See also G. W. Bowersock, *Augustus and the Greek World* (Oxford: Clarendon Press, 1965), 116.

[99] See, F. M. Abel, *Géographie de la Palestine*, Vol. II (Paris: Librairie Lecoffre, 1938), 314.

[100] See PT, Avoda Zara 5:4 44d; Joanis Moschi, *Pratum Spiritual*, cap. CLXV PG. 87, 3, 3032.

As mentioned earlier, the great victory of Augustus at Actium took place near the temple of Apollo Actius. It was believed that Apollo himself had helped Augustus defeat Cleopatra and Mark Anthony.[101] In honor of the victory, the old sanctuary of Apollo Actius was enlarged, Nicopolis was founded nearby and quinquennial games were instituted in the new city.[102] In 27 BCE Augustus gave monumental expression to his gratitude by erecting the great temple to the Actian Apollo on the Palatine.[103] Thus, we may consider Nicopolis-Actium to be the city of Apollo.

As we have seen above, it was believed in Rome that Octavian-Augustus was sired by Apollo, who visited his mother Attia in a form of a dragon. Hence, we may conclude that it is Apollo who is described in the *Book of Zerubbabel* as Armilus' father and as the lord of Nicopolis.

Now we can appreciate the polemic of the author of the *Book of Zerubbabel*. He is fully aware of Augustus' claim to divinity on the basis of his descent from the god Apollo and doesn't deny the superhuman origin of Augustus. However, for him, Augustus is the fruit of the union of Apollo-Satan with the image of the goddess Roma. In Jewish eyes, one who is sired by a dragon or serpent is a son of Satan.[104] The description of Apollo as Satan keeps both with the belief that this god was responsible for pestilence, plagues and disasters,[105] and with the image of Augustus as 'Apollo the Tormentor' discussed above.

Why is Augustus called Romulus-Armilus? Here we should look at another element in the Augustan propaganda. Augustus represented himself as a second Romulus.[106] Before he was called Augustus, it was proposed to name him Romulus.[107] Virgil also expresses the

---

[101] See Propertius, *Elegies* 4. 6. 27 (Cambridge, Mass.: Loeb Classical Library, 1990).

[102] See, Suetonius, *Augustus*. 18; Strabo 7, 7, 6; J. Gaje, 'Apollon impérial, garant des 'Fata Romana,' *ANRW* 2, 17 2 (1981): 563, n. 1.

[103] On this temple see, P. Zanker, *The Power of Images in the Age of Augustus* (Ann Arbor: University of Michigan Press, 1990), 85–89.

[104] See, I. Knohl, 'Cain: Son of God or Son of Satan,' 46–47.

[105] See, J. Fontenrose, *Python – A Study of Delphic Myth and Its Origins* (Berkeley: University of California Press, 1980), 471.

[106] See, K. Scott, 'The Identification of Augustus with Romulus-Quirinius,' *TAPA* 56 (1925): 82–125; J. Gaje, 'Romulus-Augustus,' *MEF* 47 (1930): 138–181; D. Kienast, *Kaiser Augustus: Prinzeps und Monarch* (Darmstadt: Wissenschaftliche Buchgesellschaft, 1982), 79–80.

[107] Suetonius, *Augustus*, 7; Scott, 'The Identification of Augustus with Romulus-Quirinius,' 84–85; Taylor, *The Divinity*, 158.

connection between Augustus and Romulus.[108] The author of the *Book of Zerubbabel* does not deny Augustus' claim to superhuman origin, but argues that he is the son of Satan.

Thus, the roots of the *Book of Zerubbabel* go back to the first century BCE. This may also explain the direct linguistic connection between the *Book of Zerubbabel* and *The Gabriel Revelation* noted in the first chapter.[109]

6. Conclusion: Augustus, the Antichrist

The 'Antichrist'[110] is a human being who claims to be of divine origin; hence he calls himself the 'son of God' but actually he is the son of perdition, or the son of Abaddon-Satan. He is worshiped like a god, but is a pretender and a deceiver who is presented as a savior while actually being a destroyer. His power and dominion derive from his evil descent.

In my view, the Antichrist myth developed as a result of the clash between the Jews and the foreign rulers. The first stage is to be seen in the description of Antiochus IV in the Book of Daniel,[111] but there we only find the claim to divinity. Antiochus IV made a claim to divinity but neither used titles that could be seen by the Jews as messianic nor presented himself as the savior of humanity. The impulse to the formation of the Antichrist myth emerged with the rule of Augustus.

The rise of Augustus and his claim to divinity and worship, as well as his appearance as a savior and the 'son of God,' posed a serious challenge to the Jews. The 'signs' of Augustus, the comet and the Capricorn, were minted on his coins and used everywhere in the Roman Empire. Herod was one of the great supporters of the imperial cult. The effect of the Augustan propaganda would have

---

[108] See, J. R. Fears, *The Divine Election of the Emperor as a Political Concept at Rome* (Rome: American Academy at Rome, 1977), 124–125.

[109] See chapter 1, nn. 41–42.

[110] As is well known, the term first appears in John's Epistles. However, I am using this late term here as a designation of earlier appearances of the figure.

[111] See McGinn, *Antichrist*, 26–27.

been well felt by Jews who lived in the Empire. The Antichrist myth is a response to this challenge.

The violent clash in 4 BCE between the Roman army of Augustus and the Jewish rebels ended with the killing of the messianic leaders of the rebellion. Augustus, the Roman savior and 'Son of God,' killed the Jewish messiahs who wished to redeem their people. It is no wonder then that following the cruel crushing of the rebellion and the killing of the messianic leaders, the Jews depicted Augustus as the wicked Antichrist.

In the post-Augustan period we witness an interesting process. On the one hand, Augustus' titles in the Qumranic document, the 'son of God' and 'son of the Most High,' are applied to Jesus in the Gospel of Luke.[112] On the other hand, the figure of Augustus-as-Antichrist, detached from its original historical context, became the model for the figure of the Antichrist in 2 Thessalonians. Thus, the figure of Augustus influenced the formation of the images of both the Christian Messiah and the Antichrist!

---

[112] Luke 1:32, 35. On the connection between Augustus as *divi filius* and Jesus as the Son of God see A. Deissman, *Light from the Ancient East* (London: Hodder & Stoughton, 1927), 346–347; A. Yarbro Collins, 'Mark and His Readers: The Son of God among Greeks and Romans,' *HTR* 93 (2000): 85–100.

Chapter 4

The Gabriel Revelation and the Birth of Christianity

1. The 'Messianic Secret'

According to the tradition of the synoptic Gospels, Jesus kept the knowledge of his messianic mission to himself. The first occasion on which Jesus revealed this mission to his disciples is recorded in chapter 8 of the Gospel of Mark:[1]

> He asked his them [his disciples], 'But who do you say that I am?'
> Peter answered him, 'You are the Christ!'
> And he charged them to tell no one about him.
> And he began to teach them that the Son of man must suffer many things, and be rejected by the elders and the chief priests and the scribes, and be killed, and after three days rise again.
> And he said this plainly. And Peter took him, and began to rebuke him. But turning and seeing his disciples, he rebuked Peter, and said, 'Get behind me, Satan! For you are not on the side of God, but of men.' (Mark 8:29–33)

According to the Gospels, the disciples did not comprehend Jesus' message, while he, in turn, pleaded with them to protect the secret of his unusual vision of the 'Son of man:'

> And he would not have any one know it; for he was teaching his disciples, saying to them, 'The Son of man will be delivered into the hands of men, and they will kill him; and when he is killed, after three days he will rise.' But they did not understand the saying, and they were afraid to ask him. (Mark 9:30–32)

---

[1] There are parallel traditions in Matt. 16:13–21 and Luke 9:18–22.

These stories raise a number of questions: Did Jesus consider himself to be the 'Son of man,' and, if so, why did he speak of the 'Son of man' in the third person? Was Jesus capable of foreseeing his rejection, death and resurrection? Why did Peter rebuke Jesus?

The predominant tendency in New Testament scholarship of the past hundred-odd years has been to deny the historical authenticity of these accounts. According to this view, Jesus did not regard himself as the Messiah and was not recognized as such by his disciples. Jesus, it is claimed, was unable to foresee his suffering, death and resurrection on the third day, and these presentiments were attributed to him posthumously.

This negative view of the historicity of Jesus' presaging was first formulated by W. Wrede.[2] This tack was adapted also by Bultmann who argues:

> The scene of *Peter's Confession* is no counter-evidence – on the contrary! For it is an Easter-story projected backward into Jesus' life time...[3]

Bultmann wants to confirm the conclusion that all of Jesus' predictions of his future Passion and resurrection are later fabrications, by claiming that 'the idea of a suffering, dying and rising Messiah or Son of man was unknown to Judaism ...'[4]

A similar view has been expressed in our generation by G. Vermes, who avers: 'neither the suffering of the Messiah, nor his death and resurrection, appear to be part of the faith of first-century Judaism.'[5]

Our study has revealed that this categorical assessment of first-century Judaism is misguided. It does indeed apply to the majority of Jews at the beginning of the first century CE, but not to all of them. The author of *The Gabriel Revelation*, who likely was active at the turn of the Common Era, had created a model of catastrophic messianism that was based on biblical verses. He believed that the suffering, death

---

2   W. Wrede, *The Messianic Secret*, trans. J. C. G. Greig (Cambridge and London: James Clark & Co., 1971), 82–114, 208–243.

3   R. Bultmann, *Theology of the New Testament* (New York: Scribner's Sons, 1951–55), 26.

4   R. Bultmann, *Theology*, 31.

5   G. Vermes, *Jesus the Jew* (Philadelphia: Fortress Press, 1981), 38.

and resurrection of the Messiah 'by three days' were necessary events for setting the redemptive process in motion. Hence, we should explore the possibility that the historical Jesus could have indeed foreseen the suffering, death and resurrection of the Son of man 'after three days' based on the conceptions reflected in *The Gabriel Revelation*. Our assumption has thus far been that the catastrophic messianism reflected in *The Gabriel Revelation* was formed in a circle of the followers of Simon, who was active in the Jordan area. Thus, we might suggest that Jesus could have become exposed to these ideas during his stay with John the Baptist near the Jordan.

In light of the above, it now seems that Jesus could have actually possessed a messianic secret. Thanks to the discovery of *The Gabriel Revelation*, we are able to shed new light on Jesus' walk on the path of secret messianism that lead to the Passion – death and resurrection on the third day. It emerges that Jesus of Nazareth identified with the figure of the tortured and slain messiah that he had learned of from traditions in the vein of *The Gabriel Revelation*.

Of course, the detailed version of some of the predictions, which includes the minor details of Jesus' passion, such as 'the Son of man must suffer many things, and be rejected by the elders and the chief priests and the scribes, and be killed' (Mark 8:31), cannot be ascribed to Jesus himself. These words are definitely a product of the post-crucifixion period. However, the more simple and general version of the prediction, such as 'The Son of man will be delivered into the hands of men, and they will kill him; and when he is killed, after three days he will rise' (Mark 9:31), might very well reflect Jesus' original words.

This unique messianic conception, however, was known only in the small esoteric circle of the followers of Simon, the slain messiah. Jesus' disciples were privy to it but failed to understand it: 'But they did not understand the saying, and they were afraid to ask him' (Mark 9:32). The disciples shared the common expectation for the successful and triumphal Davidic messiah. This is also why Peter was shocked by Jesus' words and rebuked him for having said them.

2. 'The Son of Joseph'

According to the genealogical lists in Matthew 1:1–16 and Luke 3:23–38, Jesus was a descendant of David. It is said explicitly about Joseph, Jesus' father, that he was 'of the house and lineage of David' (Luke 2:4 see also 1:27, 32; Matt. 1:20). Jesus is also referred to as the 'Son of David' several times in the Gospels[6] and elsewhere in the New Testament.[7] The entire Nativity story (Matt. 2:1–18; Luke 2:1–29) is devised to depict Jesus as a 'Son of David' who, like the king, was born in Bethlehem. However, Jesus himself never refers to the Messiah as the 'Son of David' and he does not mention having any link with the Davidic line.

We may find one account in the Gospels that, in my opinion, sheds light on Jesus' self-distancing from the house of David. According to the story of the Gospels, the event took place a few days before Jesus' crucifixion:

> And as Jesus taught in the temple, he said, 'How can the scribes say that Christ is the son of David? David himself inspired by the Holy Spirit, declared,
>
>> 'The Lord said to my Lord,
>> Sit at my right hand,
>> till I put thy enemies under thy feet.'
>
> David himself calls him Lord, so how is he his son?
>
> (Mark 12:35–37)[8]

According to this account, Jesus refuted the view held by the scribes that Christ, the Messiah, should be a son or descendant of David. Jesus' objection to this view, common among Jews of the period, was based on Psalm 110, which is ascribed to David. In its first verse, David addresses a person he calls 'my lord.' As Jesus opines, this person is Christ the Messiah. The very fact that David calls this person 'my lord' rather than 'my son' serves as proof that Christ is not the 'Son

---

[6]　See Mark 10:46, 11:10; Matt. 8:27, 12:23, 15:22, 20:30, 21:9; Luke 18:38.
[7]　See Rom. 1:3; Tim. 2:8; Rev. 5:5, 22:16.
[8]　See also Matt. 22:41–46; Luke 20:41–44.

of David.' This seems to indicate quite clearly that in Jesus' view Christ the Messiah is not related in any way to the house of David!

This account stands in stark contrast to the above-mentioned Gospel traditions, which claim that Jesus was Christ the Messiah and also a descendant of David. This contrast may lead us to conclude that the passage in Mark 12 is historical and authentic.[9] The authors of the Gospels would not have composed an account that clashes with their propensity to describe Jesus as the 'Son of David.'[10]

Some scholars have suggested that Jesus wished to claim that the Messiah is not merely a son of David, but rather has a superior status,[11] possibly that of the Son of God.[12] If this were the case, however, we would have expected Jesus to anchor his claim in Psalm 2:7 – 'You are my son, today I have begotten you' – rather than on the first verse of Psalm 110, which makes no explicit reference to the Messiah as the Son of God.[13]

Other scholars argue that this passage is connected to Jesus' public recognition as the son of David upon his entry into Jerusalem (Matt. 21:9. see also Mark 11:10). According to this view,[14] Jesus sought to fend off the acrimony directed at him by arguing that since the Messiah is not the son of David, he is not claiming to be the Messiah. However, this interpretation is refuted by Jesus' confession before the high priest that he is indeed the Messiah

---

[9]   For further support of the historicity of this tradition see V. Taylor, *The Gospel According to St. Mark* (London: Macmillian, 1952), 490–493. As noted by J. A. Fitzmayer, *The Gospel According to Luke X–XXIV, AB,* (New York: Doubleday, 1985), 1312, the language in which the dialogue was originally held may have been Aramaic.

[10] R. Bultmann, *History of the Synoptic Traditions* (Oxford: Basil Blackwell, 1968), 66, 136–137 has argued that the account is not historical but reflects the denial of Jesus' Davidic ancestry in a limited circle within the early Church. However, as was rightly noted by B. Chilton ('Jesus *ben David*: Reflections on the *Davidssohnfrage,*' *JSNT* 14 (1982): 102), in light of the broad consensus in the N.T. that Jesus was the son of the David, it is difficult to accept that such a circle ever existed within the early church. See further the objections of W. D. Davies and Dale C. Allison, *The Gospel According to St. Matthew, ICC,* Vol. 3 (Edinburgh: T&T Clark, 1996), 250, and R. E. Brown, *The Birth of the Messiah* (New York: Image books, 1979), 509–510.

[11] See Taylor, *The Gospel According to St. Mark,* 492; A. H. McNeil, *The Gospel According to St. Matthew* (London: Macmillan & Co, 1915), 328.

[12] See F. Hahn, *The Titles of Jesus in Christology* (London: Lutterworth, 1969), 13–15; D. Davies and Allison, *The Gospel According to St. Matthew,* 255; D. A. Hanger, *Mathew 14–28, Word Biblical Commentary* (Dallas: Word Books,1995), 651.

[13] See further the objection of J. A. Fitzmayer, *The Gospel According to Luke X–XXIV,* 1313, who claims that 'the title "Son of God" has nothing to do with this episode.'

[14] See Chilton, 'Jesus *ben David,*' 88–112.

(Mark 14:62). Other interpretations suggested for this passage[15] are not convincing.

The Gabriel Revelation attests that the figure of 'Ephraim' or the 'Messiah son of Joseph' was already known in the late first century BCE. As I have noted above, the figure of 'Ephraim' in *The Gabriel Revelation* is probably based on biblical verses depicting him as the suffering Son of God. The setting of *The Gabriel Revelation* reflects elements of mourning and exile, death and bloodshed. It appears that 'Ephraim' is a symbolic figure containing all of these elements. Unlike the messianic figure of 'David,' which traditionally represents bravery, military skill and triumph, the figure of 'Ephraim' symbolizes a very different and new type of messianism. 'Ephraim' is a messiah of suffering and death.

Thus, in light of the recent discovery of *The Gabriel Revelation*, we are able to propose a new interpretation of Jesus' commentary on Psalm 110. It is possible that Jesus sought to dispel the prevalent expectation for a triumphal messiah, the son of David. His ideal messianic model was different. Following the conception of catastrophic messianism attested to in *The Gabriel Revelation*, Jesus imagined the Messiah to be a 'Son of Joseph' or 'Ephraim' – the suffering, dead and risen Messiah.

Just as in *The Gabriel Revelation* where Ephraim is the key person who is asked to place the 'sign' and David is only the messenger, so in the saying of Jesus, David is secondary to the other Messiah.

The fact that Jesus was known in Nazareth as the 'Son of Joseph'[16] may have served as an additional catalyst for his predilection for this messianic model.

Shortly after the discussion of Psalm 110, the synoptic Gospels deliver Jesus' apocalyptic vision. According to the account in the Gospel of Matthew (24:29–30), his apocalyptic vision was worded as follows:

Immediately after the tribulation of those days the sun will be darkened, and the moon will not give its light, the stars will fall

---

[15]   See the surveys of Davies and Allison, *The Gospel According to St. Matthew*, 251; and J. Holland, *Luke 18:35–24:5*, *Word Biblical Commentary* (Dallas: Word Press, 1993), 971–972.

[16]   See Luke 4:22; John 6:42.

from heaven, and the powers of heavens will be shaken; then will appear the sign of the Son of man in heaven, and then all the tribes of the earth will mourn, and they will see the Son of man coming on the clouds of heaven with power and great glory.

We are acquainted with the motif of the darkening of the sun and the eclipse of the celestial bodies from various biblical verses;[17] the portrayal of the Son of man coming on the clouds of heaven is based on Dan. 7:13

The first part of v. 30 in this passage from Matthew is particularly relevant to our discussion:

Then the sign of the Son of man will appear in heaven, and then all the tribes of the earth will mourn.

The wording: 'then all the tribes of the earth will mourn' is based on Zech. 12:12: 'The land shall mourn, each family by itself,' which the Rabbis applied in the eulogy for the slain Messiah son of Joseph.[18]

The 'sign of the Son of man'[19] that will appear in heaven prior to the redemption is reminiscent of the depiction of 'Ephraim' in *The Gabriel Revelation*. According to our reconstruction, in lines 16–17 God addresses David, and requests that he ask Ephraim to place the sign. This placing of the sign is followed by a description of the breaking of evil and the appearance of God and the angels. *The Gabriel Revelation* is the only work known to us in which the Messiah son of Joseph places a sign heralding the advent of salvation. The tradition of the 'sign of the Son of man' might be founded on the depiction of the sign of 'Ephraim' in *The Gabriel Revelation*.

As stated above, in light of *The Gabriel Revelation*, it may be assumed that the historical Jesus had indeed foreseen the death and resurrection of the 'Son of man' after three days. Following this

---

[17] See esp. Isa. 13:10–11; 34:4; Joel 1:4.

[18] See BT Sukkah 52a; PT Sukkah 5:1 (55b).

[19] For a survey of the scholarly interpretations of the essence of this sign, see D. C. Sim, *Apocalyptic Eschatology in the Gospel of Matthew* (Cambridge: Cambridge University Press, 1996), 104–105; W. D. Davies and D. C. Allison, *Matthew, ICC* 3 (Cambridge: T&T Clark, 1997), 359–360.

argument, we may raise the possibility that the 'sign of the Son of man' is the shed blood of the Son of man, and for this reason 'all the tribes of the earth will mourn' after this sign is revealed.[20] We have seen above that according to the story of Taxo in the Testament of Moses and the catastrophic messianism in *The Gabriel Revelation,* the shed blood is the catalyst for the coming of salvation. It is possible that the same conception is present in the words of Jesus according to Matthew's account. It is only after the 'sign of the Son of man' is revealed and 'all the tribes of the earth will mourn' him, that salvation would come – 'and they will see the Son of man coming on the clouds of heaven with power and great glory.'

The three leaders of the rebellion of 4 BCE were the earliest Jewish messianic leaders of the Roman period.[21] At least two of the three messianic leaders, Simon and Athronges, were killed during the crushing of the rebellion.[22] This of course led to the question whether their death proves the falsehood of their messianic claim. In my view, the composition of *The Gabriel Revelation* was motivated by the need to resolve this conflict. The author of *The Gabriel Revelation,* who was a follower of Simon of Transjordan, developed his model of catastrophic messianism in response to this conflict. Based on the Scriptures of Daniel, he argued that the death of the Messiah is not a sign of the falsehood of the messianic claim, but rather an essential stage in the redemptive process. He believed that the dying Messiah would be resurrected by the angel Gabriel 'by three days.' In light of this conception, he also developed the image of 'Ephraim,' the suffering and dying messiah who, in his view, is superior to the triumphal Davidic messiah.

I would like to suggest that these concepts were known to Jesus. He may have become exposed to them during his stay with John the Baptist near the Jordan. This assumption might explain Jesus' presaging the suffering, death and resurrection after three days as an essential part of the redemptive process. It sheds new light on

---

[20] See Rev. 1:7, which refers explicitly to the pierced messiah. As noted by Davies and Allison, *ibid.* 360, it seems that both Matt. 24:30 and Rev. 1:7 rely on an earlier pre-Matthean tradition.

[21] See R. H. Horsley, *Bandits, Prophets and Messiahs* (Harrisburg: Continuum International, 1999), 110–117.

[22] The fate of the third leader, Judas son of Ezekias, is not clear, see Israel Knohl, 'Studies in the *Gabriel Revelation,'* *Tarbiz* 76 (2007): 322, n. 71.

Jesus' claim that the Messiah is not a son of David, as well as on the tradition of the sign of the 'Son of man' in the Gospel of Mark. Above all, it can offer an alternative understanding of Jesus' final journey to Jerusalem: if Jesus indeed shared the views of *The Gabriel Revelation*, he would have been motivated to travel to Jerusalem and to sacrifice himself in order to set the redemptive process in motion. It is only with his shed blood that he might urge God to descend on the Mount of Olives, to fight the enemies of Israel and to save his people.

Assuming this, we may gain a better understanding of the following passage depicting Jesus' last night on earth. After the last supper, Jesus went to the Garden of Gethsemane at the foot of the Mount of Olives with his disciples. There he became deeply depressed:

> And he took with him Peter and James and John, and began to be greatly distressed and troubled.
>
> And he said to them, 'My soul is very sorrowful, even to death; remain here, and watch.'
>
> And going a little farther, he fell on the ground and prayed that, if it were possible, the hour might pass from him.
>
> And he said, 'Abba, Father, all things are possible to thee; remove this cup from me; yet not what I will, but what thou wilt.'
>
> (Mark 14:33–36. Cf. also Matthew 26:36:44; Luke 22:41–44)

At this point the inner struggle within Jesus' soul reached its climax. Jesus felt that the time had come to fulfill his messianic mission, which would surely entail suffering and death. As his will to live rebelled against this fearful messianic destiny, he pleaded with his almighty Father to revoke this harsh verdict. Nevertheless, he resigned himself to what he believed to be the divine pronouncement, suspending his own will before that of God.

Jesus could have escaped his enemies under the dark mantle of the night and hidden somewhere in Galilee. But he opted to stay in Jerusalem and follow the path of suffering, death and resurrection on the third day, a messianic path devised in *The Gabriel Revelation*.

Postscript

The Gabriel Revelation is an apocalyptic text, probably composed around the turn of the Common Era. The main biblical sources on which its author relied are the second part of Zechariah and the concluding chapters of Daniel. The verses depicting Gabriel's revelation to Daniel in Daniel 8:17–27 bear a particularly strong relation to the text of *The Gabriel Revelation*. In the final section of *The Gabriel Revelation* the angel Gabriel speaks in the first person. In its opening part, the speaking voice is that of God while the identity of the addressee is not disclosed. There are points of similarity also between *The Gabriel Revelation* and the *Testament of Moses*, which was composed approximately in the same period.

The Gabriel Revelation seems to reflect the ideology of an apocalyptic-messianic group in the wake of the cruel crushing of the 4 BCE revolt. The members of this group faced tumultuous times following the killing of their messianic leader and the Roman army's vanquishing of the rebellion. It would have been only natural for an event such as the death of a messianic leader to be taken as evidence that he was a false messiah. The author of *The Gabriel Revelation*, however, seems to disqualify such a view. Based on Gabriel's address to Daniel, he probably forms an ideology of Catastrophic Messianism, according to which the defeat and death of the messianic leader and his resurrection 'by three days' form an essential part of the redemptive process. The blood of the slain messiah, expected to resurrect in three days, paves the way for the final salvation.

In *The Gabriel Revelation* we find the earliest allusion to the messianic figure of 'Ephraim'. 'Ephraim,' or the 'Messiah son of Joseph,' appears in Jewish traditions as the figure of the slain messiah. According to *The Gabriel Revelation*, it is Ephraim who has to place the 'sign' to mark the launch of the redemptive process. The essence of this 'sign' is not explained in the text. However, the context suggests that it is related to the blood of those slain by the enemy.

The Gabriel Revelation contains an Antichrist figure described as the 'wicked branch.' He bears the messianic title 'branch' but is in actual fact an 'evil branch.' The dating of *The Gabriel Revelation* suggests that this Antichrist figure may refer to Augustus, whose army banefully extinguished the revolt of 4 BCE.

Augustus' rise to power, his claim to divine status and demand of worship, as well as his presentation as a savior and the 'son of God,' posed a serious challenge to the Jews of the period. In my view, the Antichrist myth was created in response to this challenge. This polemic against Augustus is reflected also, I believe, in several other apocalyptic texts that date approximately to the same period: the Qumranic 'son of God' text, the early Jewish apocalyptic text used and redacted by the author of Revelation and the early layer of the *Book of Zerubbabel.*

There are clear linguistic parallels between the *Book of Zerubbabel* and *The Gabriel Revelation.* These may indicate that the text of *The Gabriel Revelation* was also written on scrolls and had an impact on other compositions.

The Gabriel Revelation and the other apocalyptic works of the same period suggest that the years surrounding the turn of the Common Era were pivotal to the development of apocalyptic and messianic ideology. *The Gabriel Revelation* was written near the time of Jesus' birth.

Having discovered *The Gabriel Revelation* we are able to surmise that Jesus possessed a messianic secret and thus to shed new light on Jesus' walk on the path of secret messianism leading to the Passion – death and resurrection on the third day. Jesus of Nazareth might have identified with the figure of the tortured and slain messiah that he had discovered in traditions like *The Gabriel Revelation.*

Appendix:
Further Support for the Reading:
'In three days, live'

Prof. Ronald Hendel published a letter in the last issue of *BAR* (vol. 35 no. 1 [January/February 2009], p. 8), in which he suggested reading the third word in line 80 of *The Gabriel Revelation* as האות (the sign), instead of my reading חאיה (live). I cannot accept this suggestion for two reasons:

1. The last letter of this word cannot be ת. This letter has a diagonal left leg that starts to descend before the left end of the upper horizontal line of the letter. Nowhere in this inscription is there a ת written in this way (see the shapes of ת in the table in Yardeni and Elizur's article [*Cathedra* 123 p. 164]). Thus, the reading האות can be ruled out on a paleographic basis.
2. The syntax of the sentence formed on the basis of Hendel's suggestion – לשלושת ימין האות – is problematic, as we expect to find a verb before the word האות. On the other hand, the sentence that I read לשלושת ימין חאיה is fluent and very similar in form and syntax to the sentence לשלושת ימין תדע in line 19.

The reading suggested by Prof. Hendel – האות – is thus unacceptable.

Let us now inspect all the possible readings of this word. The first letter was read as ח by Yardeni and Elizur but, since the letters ח and ה are sometimes written in a very similar way in this inscription, it might also be read as ה. The second letter is clearly א. The third letter can be either י or ו since these two letters are often undistinguishable in this inscription. As for the last letter, we earlier rejected the suggestion to read it as ת. On the other hand, we can point to two cases where the letter ה is written in a similar form, i.e. with a diagonal left leg that starts to descend before the left end of the upper horizontal line of the letter. The first example is the letter ה in the word לכה in line 21 , and the second is the letter ה in the word הצץ in line 31. In no case is the letter ח written in this form in this inscription. Hence, the last letter of this word can be read only as ה.

In conclusion, on a paleographic basis there are four possibilities for the reading of this word: האוה, חאוה, האיה and חאיה. The first three alternatives make no sense within the context of the previous and following words of this line. It is only the last possibility חאיה (live) that can be read together with the other words of this line in a meaningful way. Thus, this reading – חאיה – seems to be the only plausible reading of that word. The first words of this line should therefore be translated as following: 'In three days, live.'

Further support for the reading: לשלושת ימין חאיה 'In three days, live' can be gained from a close look at the following lines of *The Gabriel Revelation* (lines 81–85):

1. The third word of line 81 was read by Yardeni and Elitzur as ד..ן, yet, I maintain, as stated in chapter 1, that one can distinguish the top of a ו in the second letter, and the left part of a מ in the third,[1] thereby constructing the word דומן (dung). All the mentions of דמן in the Hebrew Bible are connected with people who were killed but not buried, whose bodies became 'as dung upon the earth.'[2]

2. In line 83 we read מן שלושה הקטן שלקחתי אני גבריאל 'from the three, the small one that I took, I Gabriel,' where Gabriel speaks of his taking 'the small one' of the three. The verb לקח 'take' is used in Genesis 5:24 to describe the ascension of Enoch: ואיננו כי לקח אתו אלהים 'and he was not, for God took him.' The same verb לקח 'take' is also used four times regarding the ascent of Elijah (2 Kings 2:3, 5, 9, 10). Finally, we see this verb in Psalms 49:16 (ET 15) כי יקחני סלה in a statement about a divine rescue from Sheol and death, probably by resurrection.[3]

---

1   See, for instance, the shape of the מ in מן, line 83.
2   See II Kings 9:37; Jer. 8:2; 9:21; 16:4; 25:33; Ps. 83:11.
3   See, J. Day, 'The Development of Belief in Life after Death in Ancient Israel,' in J. Barton and D. J. Reimer (eds.), *After the Exile, Essays in Honor of Rex Masson* (Macon GA, 1996), 254.

3. In line 85 we find the words אז תעמדו 'then you will stand.' The same verb עמד 'stand' is used twice in the Hebrew Bible as a reference to resurrection (Ezekiel 37:10; Daniel 12:13).

We may thus conclude by stating that lines 81–85 of *The Gabriel Revelation* contain various elements and expressions that have a clear connection to the realm of death, resurrection and ascension. Hence, my reading and interpretation of the previous line, line 80, as a reference to resurrection in three days fits very well the atmosphere and context of this part of *The Gabriel Revelation*.

Photographs

Photo 1 As pictured here, the stone is broken into three pieces. One can see that the bottom of the stone is darker than the rest, having a brown tone. This might point, in the author's view, to the fact that the stone was probably stuck in the earth, possibly serving as a memorial. One also notices that the bottom piece has no writing and that the upper right corner is broken off and missing

PHOTO 2   The Gabriel Stone, top right to line 6

Photo 3 The Gabriel Stone, lines 7–15

Photo 4   The Gabriel Stone, lines 15–23

Photo 5 The Gabriel Stone, lines 23–32

Photo 6   The Gabriel Stone, lines 31–39

Photo 7 The Gabriel Stone, lines 37–44

Photo 8 The Gabriel Stone, lines 44–end

Photo 9 The Gabriel Stone, top left

PHOTO 10   The Gabriel Stone, top to line 51

Photo 11   The Gabriel Stone, lines 51–60

Photo 12   The Gabriel Stone, lines 60–68

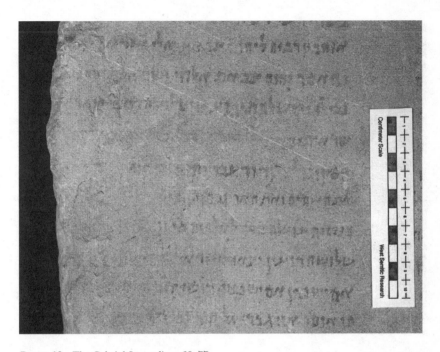

Photo 13   The Gabriel Stone, lines 68–77

PHOTO 14   The Gabriel Stone, lines 76–83

Photo 15   The Gabriel Stone, lines 82–87

PHOTO 16   This photo was taken by Mr. Arye Jeselsohn, the brother of Dr. David Jeselsohn who owns the stone, during the author's visit to Zurich. The photo shows the author reading the inscription. Behind the author stand Dr. David Jeselsohn and his wife Jemima

Bibliography Related to
The Gabriel Revelation

Bar Asher, M. 'On the Language of the Vision of Gabriel.' *Revue de Qumrane* 92 (2008): 492–524.

Goren, Y. 'Micromorpholic Examination of the *Gabriel Revelation* Stone.' *Israel Exploration Journal* 58 (2008): 220–229.

Knohl, Israel. 'On "the Son of God," Armilus and Messiah Son of Joseph.' [In Hebrew] *Tarbiz* 68 (1998): 13–38.

— *The Messiah before Jesus*. Berkeley: The University of California Press, 2000.

— 'Studies in the Gabriel Revelation.' [In Hebrew] *Tarbiz* 76 (2007): 1–26.

— 'In three days, you shall live.' *Haaretz*, 19 April 2007.

— 'The Messiah Son of Joseph.' *Biblical Archeology Review* 34:5 (2008): 58–62.

— 'By Three Days Live,' Messiahs, Resurrection and Ascent to Heaven in '*Hazon Gabriel*,' *The Journal of Religion* 88 (2008): 147–158.

Rendsburg, G. A. ' Linguistic and Stylistic Notes to the Hazon Gabriel Inscription,' *Dead Sea Discoveries* 16 (2009): 107–116.

Yardeni, A. 'A New Dead Sea Scroll on Stone?' *Biblical Archeology Review* 34:1 (2008): 60–61.

—and Elitzur, B. 'Document: A First–Century BCE Prophetic Text Written on a Stone: First Publication.' [In Hebrew] *Cathedra* 123 (2007): 55–66.

Index of Terms

Index of Scripture

The Old Testament

The New Testament